CHAPTER ONE

INNOVATION & ENTREPRENEURSHIP IN THE NEW NORMAL

Innovation is something new which could relate to a process, product or an idea. It could also relate to the new type of uses of a product or service. Innovation could involve any new technology, process or the use of existing technology in different way which was not used earlier. When any new innovative idea or technology is applied and adopted successfully in the business and results in a successful product or service accepted by the market it could be said that the innovation is successful. Lot of new ideas come to the mind of the innovators but not all of them result in successful products. Lot of ideas come into the mind of the innovators but all new products and services do not become successful. Despite all the efforts some of the products are not accepted in the market.

The following are the examples of some of the products developed by the Companies which despite all good intentions could not be successful in the Market place.

Sipani Automobiles

Sipani Automobiles Ltd. Was the manufacturer of Dolphin cars in India. The first Dolphin car that arrived in the market was in the year 1982.The Car was light in weight because of a fibre body and compact in dimension. Being light and compact it was fast too. The other Car manufacturers during that period were Premier Automobiles and Hindustan Motors. Maruti cars were also entering to market during that time. All the other Competitors of Sipani were manufacturing cars with metal body. Despite the initial euphoria and bookings it could not sustain for a longer period in the market. The buyers were not confident of a car which had plastic body and two doors.

Hero Honda Street

Hero Honda in the year 1997 launched a new bike in the name of Hero Honda Street in India .It was based on the other popular 100cc engine models of the company available in India. It had the advanced auto clutch technology where the rider of the bike was not required to depress the clutch of the bike while changing the gears. The bike had no clutch lever. While shifting the gears the clutch gets compressed and decompressed automatically. However the bike was not accepted much in the market due to the look of the motorcycle which had the design of a Moped and as a result had to be discontinued.

Thus in order to be successful in the market the innovation should be acceptable by the consumers and should not be way ahead of its time.

According to the definition of Schumpeter an entrepreneur is a person who is willing and able to convert a new idea or invention into a successful innovation. In the last century and also during the current century some innovations have changed the way people think and act. They have also increased the size of the market. Some inventions during the last century like the invention of electricity, motor cars and aeroplanes have changed the people's lives and the way of seeing the world. These innovative products besides helping the entrepreneurs to have a name and fame for themselves has also helped the economy and the Society.

During the last Century combinations of innovative and highly technical products and services like computers, internet and smart phones have helped the entrepreneurs to expand their business operations beyond the boundary of a single country to a larger market .The technology closed the doors for some entrepreneurs whereas it opened the opportunity for some others. The expansion of market and the unrestricted availability of products beyond the boundaries gave the consumers more options than ever before and the consumers understood their importance. For example if we look into the automobile market during the 1970s and 1980s in India then we can see that to get a Car or a two wheeler during that period a consumer had to wait for months and sometimes the waiting period was even higher. However this is not the case in the present era. And the COVID-19 Pandemic also taught the newer ways of doing Business. A Customer willing to buy a vehicle can do all the activities like booking a vehicle and making payment online and can have a contactless delivery too.

The addition of various online payment gateways not only helped the entrepreneurs to have a better reach in the market but also helped the customers to buy products with ease without going to the physical stores. The payment gateway in addition to the high speed internet is an important innovation of the current century. Technology has played a greater role in innovation. Computers with superior computing powers and the advent of newer and better software aided by digital technology led to the advent of a number of mobile applications to be used by customers in their smart phones .This in turn created more business .With the addition of technology the concept of marketing the products and services have also changed. Through technology it is possible for the Business to get into the mind of the customers .Thus e-marketing has replaced door to door marketing.

Technology has not only helped the product market but also has helped the service sector in introducing new way of providing services. There have been a number of innovations in the service sector too. Taxi Services like Ola and Uber, food delivery services like Swiggy and Zomato, payment gateways like Phonepe and Google pay had successfully demonstrated the use of technology in the service sector.

However no innovation is permanent and there is always a better way of doing it. It today's world of constant innovation there is always a room for improvement and there is a constant threat from competitors. So entrepreneurs must keep on innovating through research & development. Because a shift in the preference of consumers can create problems for some companies. Mobile Handset sector is an example in this direction. In the beginning of this Century mobile handsets became affordable and it became a way of communication as telecom service providers created networks for communication. Keypad handsets initially ruled the market and some companies became the household name. However as soon as the touch screen phone market came into existence and a combination of platforms like Android,IOS and 4G mobile networks changed the market equations. Another set of Companies replaced the existing market leaders due to change in people's preference coupled with new technology. Change in technology also changed the equation in the mobile service providers. People preferred those companies which provided better services and additional facilities. Thus no change and innovation is permanent and those entrepreneurs who think of innovation and change as a continuous process can win over the heart of the customers.

At times change and innovation results from the action and reaction of the Government and Society. Worldwide protest against environmental pollution necessitated the decrease in the manufacturing of diesel cars. Those Companies which could not provide alternative solutions like a good petrol engine car to replace their diesel powered car saw a decrease in their market share. Similarly the Companies focussing on electric vehicles and hybrid vehicles combining the power of gasoline and electricity gained their importance in the market.

Sometimes chance factors also affect the process of innovation and it gives rise to a new breed of entrepreneurs who would not have become successful otherwise. The current worldwide pandemic resulting from COVID-19 shows how chance factors could result in successful innovations. For example take the case of education sector . It was the assumption of the people associated with education sector that class room teaching is the best way for academic delivery. However some people associated in this sector had already started the online mode of delivery of course. Those who were prepared for online delivery of courses and were ready with the course content and course material reaped the benefit during the Pandemic. Online meeting platforms like Zoom, Google Meet,Impartus also proved their market readiness as an intermediary between teachers and students, corporate and clients and showed that there is always a way if there is a will.

Thus innovation is a way of continuation of Business for an entrepreneur. The current pandemic resulting from COVID-19 is not the only challenge faced by the human race .Various wars and other calamities like natural calamities and diseases have threatened the human race time and again. We have to use our intellect to overcome these challenges. The current pandemic possess short –term challenges but also opens up some incredible opportunities for the future. Organizations and individuals those who are prepared to embrace the change and seize the opportunity will have a higher likelihood of success and market dominance.

The entrepreneurs must find the areas of opportunity. The problems faced by the human race in present time will not be there forever .But the solutions will teach us how to act intelligently in future. The following are some of the focus areas for entrepreneurship.

-Robotics and Automation will be the focus area

-Businesses like Mobile Payments and Online Meeting Platforms

-E-Learning is not a new concept but till now has been the secondary method of education.

Some of the Successful innovations

1. Cavinkare and Chik Shampoo

C.K. Ranganathan, Chairman and Managing Director of Cavinkare, a Rs 500-crore cosmetics company, wanted to fulfill the dreams of his father Chinni Krishnan, a school teacher by profession who wanted to make products affordable to common man.He switched to the pharmaceutical packaging business and tried innovations in it. He put talcum powder in sachets but did not succeed. But according to Ranganathan his father sowed the seed of the sachet revolution and he learnt his first business lessons from his father. After splitting from his brothers' shampoo-manufacturing business, run under the brandname Velvette, Ranganathan bought a shampoo packaging machine and with an initial investment of Rs 15,000, launched Chik Shampoo, named after his father Chinni Krishnan. He sold 20,000 sachets in the first month, making a modest profit. According to Ranganathan the journey was bumpy and banks refused loans as I could not offer collateral.

He started the Chik India Company in 1982 and did the unthinkable by launching shampoos in rural, instead of urban areas. If MNC-bottled shampoos found shelf space in departmental stores, Cavinkare peddled its Re-1 wonder through roadside shops and grocery outlets in rural areas. Corporations soon realised the power of the sachet and launched their own products in small, affordable packages.

After capturing the Tamil Nadu market, Ranganathan organised village tours and conducted live demonstrations in movie halls on the use of shampoos. Soon enough, villagers replaced body soap for hair wash with the Re-1 sachet. Cavinkare then launched Shikakai powder, talcum powder, hair oil and fairness cream in sachets infusing beauty consciousness among rural masses, also showing a multi-crore possibility to other companies.

2. **OYO Rooms**

Ritesh Agarwal is an Indian Entrepreneur and founder CEO of OYO Rooms.He was born in Bisam Cuttack and brought up in Titilagarh,both places being in the State of Odisha,India.At the age of 13 he started selling SIM Cards of mobile phones.Agarwal was dropped out of College and was selected for Peter Thiel Fellowship.The fellowship is intended for School dropouts under the age of 23 and it offers them a fellowship of US$1,00,000 over a period of two years.Ritesh belongs to a family running a small local shop in Odisha.He was not good at study.So he thought if he goes to college and don't do well then his Family may not like it.So he decided to start some entrepreneurial venture instead.He founded the Company before the age of 20.Ritesh funded his entrepreneurial activity through the venture capital funds.Initially he raised a total of US$125 million in four rounds from 7 investors.OYO rooms has a network of 2,200 hotels operating in 154 cities across India with a monthly revenue of US$3.5 million and 20,000 employees.It's current valuation is US$10 billion which makes it one of the most valuable start-ups in India after financial services firm Paytm and e-commerce giant Flipkart.

3. 3M

Minnesota Mining and Manufacturing Company was founded by Dr. J. Danley Budd, Henry. S. Bryan, William A. McGonagle, John Dwan and Hermon W. Cable in Two Harbours, MN. in the year 1902. The Company's name was changed to 3M in the year 2002.In the year 2014 3M reached an innovation milestone with the issuance of its 100,000th patent. Each year about 3,000 patents are issued to 3M worldwide, with more than 500 granted in the U.S. Post– it and Scotch Brite are amongst its well-known products. It earns revenue of more than US $ 5 billion.

4. Honda Super Cub

Honda Super Cub, a 50cc motorbike was conceived by Soichiro Honda of Honda Motors in the year 1956.Takeo Fujisawa, partner of Soichiro Honda had in his mind to introduce a moped in the Company's line up for the expansion of Business. Honda along with Fujisawa was on a trip to Europe to win the Isle of Mann TT Race. During their visit to Europe they visited the Lambretta and Kreidler showrooms to get some idea regarding the future products of Honda Company. However both of them realized that a small wheeled scooter will not suit the Japanese Market because of the road conditions as well as the requirements of the market. Till now the Company had in its product range large capacity motorcycles which required higher cost and maintenance and was not meant for the mass market.Fujisawa wanted that Honda should design a product that should appeal to the masses and at the same time will require less maintainance.Also the product should be easy to use and it could almost be operative in single hand. Keeping all these points in mind Soichiro Honda developed the Honda Super Cub which became popular in Japanese market. And Honda Super Cub debuted in Japanese Market in the year 1958.

Following the route of overseas market expansion Honda Company sent Kihachiro Kawashima and his assistant to U.S.A. to study the motorcycle market in U.S.A. and the possibility of selling their existing 250 cc motorcycle in the US Market. Japan that time was a resource starved country emerging from the miseries of the World War II. Due to shortage of funds Kawashima and his assistant was using the smaller capacity Honda Cub while making rounds to visit the motorcycle dealers in order to save money.Kawashima found that their existing bigger 250 cc motorcycle is not suitable to the US market. He found that Bikers in USA prefer Harley-Davidson and Indian because of the built quality and the maintenance cost. However both the Honda employees observed that peoples are getting attracted to the Honda Cub bike and even the motorcycle dealers expressed their desire to sell the Honda Cub. After much hesitation and after final discussion with the top management of Honda it was decided that Honda Cub will be sold in USA. An advertising campaign was created and a simple slogan was used "You meet nicest people on a Honda". Honda tasted success in the overseas market with the successful launch of Honda Cub in the US market and gradually increased market share to 63%.

The Super Cub story teaches that an Entrepreneur must always be open to suggestions and the market Survey and feedback plays a vital role in introducing a new product and service in the market. The entrepreneur must use the market feedback to develop and design new products and Services. Further while designing a product choice and taste of the consumers, use of technology, Govt. regulations should be kept in mind.

5.Timex Watches

In the 1950s the United States Timex Corporation introduced its line of inexpensive pin-lever Timex watches in the US Market and

the competitors did not took notice of it .Twenty Years later the Timex Brand had sales of US$ 200 million, plants all over the world and 17,000 employees.
So what was the success strategy of Timex and how it attained?

Let us first of all have an understanding of the US watch market during the 1950s.During that time Jewellers were the main sellers of watches and were selling expensive watches on which they were getting good margins. Thus when Timex approached the Jewellers they were reluctant to handle the Timex watches .The reasons cited by the Jewellers were that it's a simple pin lever watch and it has a low price range .The Timex watches were available at a price range of less than $ 50 in the US market. Others cited fewer margins as the reason for their reluctance. As a result of this reluctance shown by the Jewellers to sell the Timex Brand of watches the Company Management looked for other channels of distribution. As a result of this the Company started marketing it's watches directly through 20,000 retail stores of which 80% consists of drug stores. Over the years the number of these retail outlets increased to 2, 50,000 and a majority of these retail stores consisted of drugstores, hardware stores and tobacco stores.

The Timex watches introduced in the 1950s were basically men's watches available at a price range of $6.95 to $7.95.Their line up caught the attraction of the public as they were simple yet modern looking and styled tastefully. This represented an innovation as no such line of watches was available at that price range. Gradually Timex introduced more features in their products like shockproof, waterproof and anti-magnetic with a higher price at $12.95.Further Timex introduced its line of women's watches. And in the early sixties it had more than 36% of market share of the US under $50 women's watch market. In order to boost the market share Timex resorted to advertising Campaigns. Initially Timex's Advertising was limited to magazines and later shifted to network television. It demonstrated many tortured tests on which the watches were shown ticking away after being fastened to galloping horses, airplanes and engine Propellors.The Company wanted to give the message that these watches are for active people and it can survive in any environment. Further Timex Salesmen visiting retailers slammed the watches into the walls and immersed them into waters to show their ability to be shockproof and waterproof. In addition to innovative advertising policy it followed a simple yet strict production formula which was based on standardisation of parts used, maximum mechanization and centralised quality control. The combination of aggressive pricing policy, manufacturing and mass distribution capability and intensive advertising campaign helped Timex to be a market leader in the low priced watch segment.

CHAPTER TWO

Qualities of an Entrepreneur

Entrepreneurship has been defined in various ways. The word entrepreneurship is derived from the French word Entreprendre which means to undertake i.e. the person who undertakes the risk of new enterprise. The word entrepreneur first appeared in the French language in the beginning of the sixteenth country. And it was first used by Richard Cantilon, an Irishman living in France who first used the term entrepreneur to refer to economic activities.
Thus entrepreneurship is basically and often associated with a person who starts his own new and small business. Business encompasses manufacturing, transport, trade and all other self-employed vacations in the service sector.
Various authors have defined Entrepreneur and Entrepreneurship some of which are as follows:
Cantilon defines Entrepreneur as a person who buys factor services at certain prices with a view to selling its product at certain prices.
The New Encyclopaedia Britannia considers an entrepreneur as an individual who bears the risk of operating a business in the face of uncertainty about the future conditions.

According to F.H. Knight entrepreneurs are a specialized group of persons who bears risks and deal with uncertainty.

Joseph A. Schumpeter defines entrepreneur as a person one who innovates, raises money assembles inputs, chooses managers and sets the organization going with his ability to identify them.
Innovation could occur through
-The introduction of a new quality in a product
-A new product itself

-Discovery of a fresh demand and a fresh source of supply and
-By changes in the organization and management

Schumpeter adds that in a developing economy an entrepreneur is a person who starts an industry, it could either be old or new, undertakes risk, bears uncertainties and also performs the managerial functions of decision-making and coordination and puts the new process based on analogical research into operation.

However in order to be successful an entrepreneur must have the following four positive attributes.

Innovativeness- It means the Entrepreneur must bring innovation to the product or service or new ways of using the product or service.

Risk taking Ability-All entrepreneurs have to deal with some or other type of risk. Thus they must have the ability to deal with some degree of uncertainty or risk associated with their venture.

Vision – They should have the ability to foresee the state of things through their intelligence. Through Vision an Entrepreneur can take his Organization to greater heights.

Organizing skills -They must have the ability to deal with larger set of things and people.

Characteristics of an Entrepreneur

-Willingness to work hard distinguishes successful Entrepreneurs from an unsuccessful one. It is an important characteristic of an Entrepreneur.

-He must have an interest for High Achievement

-Being Highly optimistic is another important Characteristics of an Entrepreneur

- Must have the capability and willingness to take decisions independently.

- He should have a good foresight. It means he must be in a position to estimate the demand for his products and services.

- Being a Good organizer is another important characteristic of an Entrepreneur.

- Being Innovative is very important. A number of people who are very successful entrepreneurs have developed very innovative products.

Various Stages in the Entrepreneurship Process

I. Idea generation and scanning for the best suitable idea

This is the first step in any entrepreneurship process. Idea generation involves deciding about the selection of a new project. The project could involve something relating to a product or service which is already there or it could be a completely new idea. For example if we talk about bringing innovation to an existing line of product then we could talk about shampoo industry. In the 1980s' a southern based Company started distributing shampoos in sachets which concept was a very new one.

On the other hand innovation could result due to introduction of a new product or service which was not there in the market.

II. Product analysis and Market Research

Before entering into any entrepreneurship venture it is very important to make a proper analysis of the new product. For this purpose it is very important to conduct market research. Corporates at times uses the tool of Market Research to relaunch an existing product.

III. Determination of form of ownership/organization

Determination of the Form of Organization is a very important step in the entrepreneurship process. Although at initial stage one can opt for the sole proprietorship type of Organisation where one person forms the Organization and takes all the decisions relating to the organization it is always advisable to go for a limited liability Company. Depending upon the number of promoters, area of operation and the requirement of funds the type of Organization could either be a Public Limited Company or a Private Limited Company. Further in case it is a non-profit organization then it could also be registered under section 25 of the Companies Act, 1956.

IV. Completion of promotional formalities

Promotional formalities involve deciding about the name of the Company, name of the promoters, place at which registered office will be situated. All these information are registered with the Registrar of Companies/ Registrar of Societies depending upon the type of Organization selected. Further in case of Company form of organization suitability regarding listing in stock exchanges are to be decided.

V. **Raising necessary funds** - It is another important aspect of entrepreneurial process. To convert one's dream into reality one need the requisite amount of funds. Where and how to get funds depends on the size of the project and the reach of the entrepreneur. Various sources of funds include one's own savings; taking loan from spouse and relatives is another option. In some cases depending on the strength of the project it is possible to obtain bank loan. Venture Capital is another source from which funds could be arranged. Various Govt.agencies too could be approached for this purpose.

VI. **Procurement of men, machine and material-** Recruitment of requisite men for running the organization,adoption of necessary and updated technology and process and use of quality material is another important aspect of entrepreneurship process.

VII. **Undertaking the business operations**-It is important to start the business operations at the earliest. No idea remains new for a longer period of time. In due course competition comes up. A number of ideas which have been successful in the past have always been copied. So in order to have the first mover advantage it is necessary to begin business operations and getting advantages out of it.

VIII. **Managing the business operation** – There is always a difference between the projected figures and the reality. Sometimes there are teething problems. At other times some problems arises which might not have been foreseen earlier. This could occur due to change in govt.policy,change in public policy and attitude of the public. Thus it is important for any entrepreneur to understand the technicalities of the business operations. At times because of perfect timing and business acumen some people build great business operations whereas others may not sustain it. Classic example is that of Reliance Industries.When the cloth mills of Mumbai were collapsing and becoming sick Dhirubhai Ambani successfully established his business operations.

Types of Entrepreneurs – All the entrepreneurs do not think and act alike. Entrepreneurs can be categorised into various categories.Some of which could be as follows:

Innovative Entrepreneurs: Innovative Entrepreneurs are those entrepreneurs who introduce new products, methods or technology etc.Steve Jobs,the founder of apple computers comes under this category as he is widely recognized as a person who pioneered the personal computer revolution.He changed the the way people think about mobile phones too.

Adaptive or initiative Entrepreneurs: These entrepreneurs always show their readiness to adopt successful innovations. They initiate the techniques and technology innovated by others. When Apple and Samsung became successful in smart phone business others quickly entered into this line of business to take the advantage of the people's rising demand for this products.

Fabian Entrepreneurs : These are characterized by those Entrepreneurs who show great caution and skepticism in experimenting any change in their enterprise. They initiate only when it becomes perfectly clear that failure to do so would result in a loss of the relative position in the enterprise.Nokia is an example in this case. For a certain period of time Nokia was a dominant player in the mobile handset market. However after the advent of the smart phones adoption of technology played a very important role. Whereas some players in the handset market used android operating system others like Apple and Blackberry adopted their own operating systems. However due to no clear-cut policy statement at the top level the market share of Nokia fell down. Then Nokia adopted the popular operating system to make a comeback.

Drone Entrepreneurs: They are characterized by their refusal to adopt opportunities to make changes in the production formula even at the cost of severely reduced returns relative to other like producers. Such entrepreneurs may even suffer from heavy losses but yet they are not ready to make changes in their existing production methods. Two classic cases can be that of Blackberry mobile handset and Hindustan Motors.

Solo operators: Solo Operators are those entrepreneurs who prefer to run their business on their own and grow a business without emloyees.Mike Geary is an example of solo entrepreneur. He is considered as one of the smartest online marketers in the world. His e-book "The Truth About Six-Pack Abs" has sold more than 5,00,000 copes since 2005.He publishes a fitness and health Newsletters to about 6,80,000 subscribers and act as a media buyer. All the three components of his business generate about US $ 1 million per month.

Active Partners: Active Partners are those entrepreneurs who take active interest and participate actively in any business venture unlike passive or sleeping partners who prefers to stay away from the active business operations but participate in profits only. Active partners on the other hand act as an active member in the board of directors or top management and gets involved in the day-to-day running of the business.

Inventors: Inventors are those entrepreneurs who do not get satisfied with only one product invention .They continuously try to invent new products and innovate their product lines. They also continuously try to bring innovation in their existing product or service line. Big Corporations like Sony, 3M continuously work towards new inventions and innovations.

Buyers: Buyers are those categories of entrepreneurs who do not prefer to do the initial hard work of setting up an enterprise and running it. Rather they prefer to buy and existing and running business through the take-over route.

Life timers: Entrepreneurs falling in this category do not rest even if the project is successful. They take it as an integral part of their life. People running family business fall into this category.

We could also Classify Entrepreneurs into the following Categories:

Further Classification of Entrepreneurs according to the types of Business conducted by them
Trading Entrepreneur

Trading Entrepreneurs are those who engage themselves in trading activities. They could further be classified as follows:

-Wholesale Traders are those whose main business is bulk trading in wholesale.

-Retail Traders are those who set up shops and do the retail trading

-Exporters are those entrepreneurs whose main business is to export goods to some other country for making profit.

-Importers are those who import goods from some other foreign country and do the trading or supply of those goods to make gain from it.

-Real Estate Dealers are those who who deal in land and building and make gain from doing so.

Industrial Entrepreneurs

-Large Scale Industrial Entrepreneurs are those Entrepreneurs who concentrate on setting up large scale industries.

-Medium Scale Industrial Entrepreneurs are those who invest in Industries where the annual turnover does not exceed two hundred and fifty Crore rupees and the investment in plant and machinery does not exceed rupees fifty crores.

-Small Scale Industrial Enterprises are those Industries where the annual turnover does not exceed fifty Crore rupees and the investment in plant and machinery does not exceed rupees ten crores

-Micro Sector Industrial Enterprises are those Industries where the annual turnover does not exceed five crore rupees and the investment in plant and machinery does not exceed rupees one crore.

Agricultural Entrepreneurs

Agricultural Entrepreneurs are those entrepreneurs whose main line of Business involves various products based on Agriculture. There are various products in agriculture which have good profit potentials. Their involvement could be in the areas of Plantation and Horticulture. Further they could be involved in Dairy Farming and Floriculture. Animal Husbandry, Poultry Farming are some more areas where entrepreneurs can grow.

Service Entrepreneurs: Service Sector is another sector which has a high growth potential for entrepreneurs. A number of activities could be included in it.Some of the activities which fall under the service sector include repairing jobs, various engineering services, health and wellness services and a number of other services.

Intrapreneur

Intrapreneur is an employee who works in a large corporation and with the support of the top management takes direct responsibility for turning his idea into a profitable finished product through assertive risk-taking and innovation. The intrapreneur has the same characteristics as that of the entrepreneur i.e. conviction, passion and drive. The Intrapreneur can be successful when the company becomes supportive and gives him a free hand to run his project. The Post-it note by 3M,Facebook's "like" button and Sony Play Station are examples of Intrapreneurship.Spencer Silver developed the Post-It note while working with the 3M.Andrew Corbet in his article "The Myth of the Intrapreneur" in Harvard Business Review have written that Companies need a strategic plan for professionalizing and institutionalizing innovation across their organizations. Just hiring a few talented individuals and hoping for the best without changing anything about the organization won't be useful.

CHAPTER THREE
Entrepreneurial Decision Making Process

Everyday people come out with a number of creative ideas and a few of these ideas actually see the light of the day and the resultant product or service come to the market and a new venture is created. Indeed millions of ventures are formed despite recession, inflation, high interest rates, and lack of infrastructure, economic uncertainty and high probability of failure. Each of these ventures is formed through a very personal human process that, although unique has some characterizes common to all. While some venture result from specific circumstances many entrepreneurs follow the entrepreneurial decision process, which is a movement from something in the present to something in future, i.e. a movement from the present life style to forming a new enterprise.

When an individual takes a decision to start an entrepreneurial venture he leaves a comfortable and well-traded path and instead opts for a route about which although he has some idea but is not fully aware of.

So we will discuss the factors that compel an individual to become an entrepreneur and what are the possible and desirable factors that can lead to his entrepreneurial success or failure.

Reasons for choosing Entrepreneurship as a Career
I. Change from the present life style

The decision to leave a career or a lifestyle is not an easy one. It takes a great deal of courage and energy to change and to do something new and different.

Thus an entrepreneur must be ready to accept those challenges. Entrepreneurship is not like nine to five jobs. Sometimes it becomes very demanding. An entrepreneur has to work hard and give more hours than a normal job.

II. Work Environment

Sometimes work environment encourages a person to start a new entrepreneurial venture. Two kinds of work environments are particularly useful for starting a new enterprise. These are research and development and marketing. While working in technology areas individuals develop new product ideas or processes. However when they find that new ideas are not accepted by their present employers and they are of the opinion that these ideas can be transformed into successful products they often leave their jobs to form their own companies. Similarly individuals working in the field of marketing become familiar with the various markets and customers they work with and when they do not get requisite pay rise or recognition they frequently leave companies to start their own venture.

III. Disruption in Work Environment

Sometimes disruption in the work environment propels an employee to look for entrepreneurial venture. It is a negative force that compels people to create something new and make a living out of it. Retirement, transfer and retrenchment forces people to start their own venture. There is no age limit for starting an entrepreneurship venture. Similarly if after completion of a higher degree like MBA, M. Tech, and Ph. D etc. the employee does not get the expected promotion, recognition and increase in pay packet then the employee may decide to leave his or her workplace and start a new venture.

Motivational Factors for the formation of a new venture:

There are certain factors that influence the formation of a new venture. These factors can be classified into two categories. These are (1) Desirable factors, and (2) Possible Factors

I. Desirable Factors

The perception that starting a new company is desirable results from an individual's culture, subculture, family, teachers and peers.

(a)**Culture:** A culture that values an individual who successfully creates a new business will encourage more venture formation than the one that does not. E.g. the American culture encourages all aspects of entrepreneurship, which results in high rate of company formation in countries like U.S.A.

(b)**Subculture**: Sometimes a whole country may not support the concept of entrepreneurship but a part of it may support. E.g. in India in cities like Mumbai, Bangalore there is support for entrepreneurs.

(c)**Family Traits**: Through surveys it has been found in various companies around the world that a very high percentage of the founders of companies had fathers and /or mothers who valued independence.

(d)**Teachers**: Encouragement to form a company is further stimulated by teachers, who can significantly influence individuals to regard entrepreneurship of a desirable and viable career path. E.g. IIMs, HBS, MIT, IITs etc.

(e)**Peers:** Finally peers are very important in the decision process to form a company.

II.Possible Factors

Although the desired support required from the individual culture, subculture, family, teachers and peers need to be present but to make a new venture successful several other factors like Government, Background, Marketing, Role models and Finance plays a very vital role.

(a)**Government Support**: The government's role is very important as they provide vital supports by providing infrastructure like roads, communication system, transportation system, utilities and a proper tax structure. Sometimes it is also requisite on the part of the Government to provide tax incentives, tax holidays and subsidies for start ups .Further it is also required to built SEZs/EPZs to give the boost to entrepreneurs.

(b)**Entrepreneurial Background**: Since in a new venture social, psychological and financial risks are present, the entrepreneur having a good entrepreneurial background can handle new projects in a better way. Formal education and previous business experience, give a potential entrepreneur the skills needed to form and manage a new enterprise.

(c)**Knowledge of Marketing**: An understanding of marketing skills also plays a critical role in forming a new company. In addition to the presence of a market of sufficient size there must also be a level of marketing know how to put together the best total package of product, price, distribution and promotion needed for a successful product launching.

(d)**Role Model**: A role model can be one of the most powerful influences in making company formation seem possible. If an entrepreneur has a role model who is a successful entrepreneur then he is motivated to attain the position of the Role model someday.

(e)**Financial Resources**: Finally in order to transform the planning stage to action stage financial resources must be readily available. Although most of the start up money for any new company comes from personal savings, credit, friends and relatives there is also a need for additional risk capital.

Reasons for choosing to become an Entrepreneur

Any person willing to start a business must first of all be determined to do so. Although earning money is the primary reason behind every business venture, there are other reasons too to start a business venture. Some of these are as follows:

1. Utilization of Talent –Sometimes earning money may not be the only concern for an entrepreneur. He may be interested to utilize his time and talent which he thinks has not been properly utilized.

2. To take advantage of the business situations – At times a person becomes an entrepreneur when he finds himself in a situation from which he can take advantage and make a good living out of it. For example when an employer trusts an employee and asks him to set up a business unit or manufacturing unit to supply a critical component.

3. To earn name and fame – Though the objective of entrepreneurship is moving towards the goal of self sufficiency at times this may not be the criteria for entrepreneurship. Social entrepreneurship is an area where earning money does not become the sole criteria.

4. Self-employment – Entrepreneurs choose the path of entrepreneurship because they choose to be self employed and independent and does not want to be dependent on the mercy of the employer.

5. Pain of unemployment or underemployment – At times the pain of unemployment or under employment paves the path for entrepreneurship. At times a person feels the pain of underemployment where he does not get remuneration as expected for a person having similar type of education or experience.

6. Financial security – Financial Security though is not the top priority for choosing the path of entrepreneurship but it is one of the criteria for becoming an entrepreneur.

CHAPTER FOUR

Entrepreneurial Start-Up Process

The entrepreneur is a person who sets his target to start a new project and to run it successfully. However at times it may so happen that though he is interested to start a venture but he is short of ideas. He may also be on the lookout for new ideas as the competition in the existing line of business is very high and hence the profit margin is low. New Ideas for doing business could be obtained from various sources. These include trade fairs, various national level industrial and agricultural surveys, focus areas of the Govt., import and export analysis, internet, demand supply position in the industry etc.

Step I. Do an Opportunity Analysis: Before starting a new business project one has to look at the various opportunities that are available. The following factors are to be considered while identifying and selecting a business opportunity.

- Understanding one's own capabilities, strengths, limitations and preferences. This is the first and the foremost factors to look out for. One must understand one's own Capability. For example a person may be very good at marketing skill. Similarly another person may have a capability of human relations skills .Another person may be very good at technology and computers etc.So it is very essential that a person must utilize his strong points to make the entrepreneurial ventures a successful one.
- Exploring all possible and suitable opportunities available within existing conditions and environment.
- Understanding the Broad Industry groups – Entrepreneurs may select a broad industry group like plastics, engineering, chemicals etc.

Step II. Do a Market Survey

Market Survey is a very important method to understand whether the proposed product or service which the entrepreneur intends to launch in the market will meet the expectations of the people or not. An entrepreneur has to understand his customer's behaviour, demands, desires and needs. He also must have knowledge about his existing and potential competitors and his marketing environment. In order to have a good market share and to understand the demand for his products or services the entrepreneur must have a market survey.

Before doing a market survey, it is important to define the market segment for the product/service like whether the product or service is meant for rural market, urban market, export market, teenagers market, adult's market, upper class markets etc.

The process of market survey should involve the following steps:

1. Define the Objective of the Survey –The first and foremost thing is to define the objective of the survey. It is important to understand the purpose of the survey. The purposes or objectives could be one or more than one. For example it could be launching a new product in a new market, it could be launching an existing product in an existing market or could be the relaunch of a product.

2. Identifying the Information Required Once the objective of the survey is defined the next step is to find answer to the following important aspects relevant to market survey

A. Determine the specific target market: All the products manufactured and sold in the market are not meant for everyone. For example in Malls you may find products with larger size as people living in the City having higher disposable income prefer to buy goods which can be stored for a longer period of time .However this is not the case for poor people living in villages. They need products in lesser size and denomination as they tend to buy products more frequently. Similarly an app based taxi service provider cannot provide service to all the areas. Hence it is important to find out the market segment at which the specific product or service will be targeted.

B. Find out the Substitute products- The presence of substitute products has a deeper impact on the success or failure of a product. For example tea and coffee can be considered as substitute products. So if the price of coffee increases substantially then price sensitive costumers may opt for the lower priced tea. So it it is very important to understand the nature of the product in relation to the substitute products available.

C. Calculate the Present Demand- One should have the understanding of the demand and supply position of the market before starting any entrepreneurship venture. For example if you want to set up an toothpaste manufacturing unit then you must find out the existing market share of the current players, whether people are ready to change their existing products, what new factors in your product can compel customers to shift their choice from the existing products to newer ones and what will be the uniqueness of your product.

D. Find the Break-up of present demand – The next step is to find out the present demand for the similar kind of products in different regions. A start up company may not have the resources to do the business in all regions or markets .Companies like **KFC** and **NIRMA** and a host of other companies at first have become successful in their own regions before venturing into national and international arena. For example if you are planning to start a food business then you must understand that in a country like India all the regions do not have the preference for similar type of foods. So it is very important to understand the break-ups.

E. Get Information relating to the price trends- It is a very important step and vital for the success or failure of any product or service. The entrepreneur must be sure about his target customers. If the targeted customers are price sensitive ones then the entrepreneur must price the product according to the nature of the product unless he can be justify about the uniqueness of the product in case of higher pricing. For example the price of a cup of tea from a local roadside vendor and a restaurant will vary and more prices can be charged for masala tea, cardamom tea etc.

F. Measure the Degree and nature of competition – If your product or service is something which is much personalised or technologically so advanced or patented that there is no competitor then you can enjoy a good a good market share and profit. However this type of situation occurs very rarely as for every product or service some sort of competition is bound to occur. Hence one must have a complete list of major competitors, their product range, product features output, market share and pricing.Futher one must have the knowledge about the new and upcoming enterprises about to begin production or about to provide service. Further it Important to have the information regarding import statistics relating to that product. Further one has to see if there is any Cartel among existing producers. One more factor to be considered is what are the present channels of distribution and mode of payment of commission to middlemen

Step III. Fulfil the Legal Requirement- Before starting up any business organisation one must fulfil the legal obligations to set up the business and industrial venture. The following legal requirements have to be complied with for this purpose.

1. SSI Registration –If the unit to be set up comes under the definition of small scale industries then it has to be registered as per the guide lines for such units.

2. Acquisition of Land and Building for the Unit- If the Business involves manufacturing of products then in that case acquisition of land and buildings becomes an integral aspect. In other cases where the entrepreneurship is related to any service industries then depending on the availability of funds office space could either be acquired through purchase or on rent.

3. Obtaining Pollution control clearance from Govt. Agencies- This is very important step without which it is not possible to start any industry. Before starting any manufacturing unit one must follow the requisite guidelines relating to the location of the industry and type of industrial effluents coming out of that plant.

4. Decision regarding Type of company – An entrepreneur has to take decision relating to the formation of type of Company. Here two things must be taken into account. First of all controlling stake in the Company should not be diluted. At the same time capital arrangement must be adequate taking into account the present operations and future expansion of business.

Step IV. Arrangement of finance – Finance must be arranged both for fixed assets and current assets. While deciding about the sources from which the funds are to be obtained, the entrepreneur must keep in mind the following points:

- Cost of borrowing
- Period for which funds are needed
- Time taken to obtain money
- Purpose for which funds are needed
- Repayment capacity

Internal source from which funds could be arranged include the following:

- Own savings
- Personal loan from LIC, Provident funds etc.
- Persona borrowing from friends, relatives
- Money raised through mortgage of shares, lands etc.

External Sources from which funds could be arranged include the following:

- Long-term Loans from Banks and financial Institutions
- Short-term loans for financing current assets
- Plant Leasing
- Hire Purchase
- Issuance of Equity Capital through Initial Public Offering
- Obtaining funds through Venture Capital
- Arrangement with Banks for Overdraft
- Commercial bills

CHAPTER FIVE

Understanding the Basic Management Concepts

HUMAN RESOURCE MANAGEMENT
Organizations are run by individuals and they are the human assets through which all other assets are utilized. Management of human resource is a specialized task and cannot be achieved automatically. Hence management of human resource is an important aspect of management.

Meaning of HRM
Human resources not only include the number of persons employed in an Organization but also include their skill, knowledge, talent, ability, creativity, aptitude etc. present in the man power. Management of resources of the individuals is the HRM which includes forecasting, planning, organizing, directing, coordination and controlling the activities of human resources for the implementation of plans and programs of an organization. HRM is also a process of hiring and utilizing the right kind of manpower for achieving the organizational goal.

Functions of HRM
Human resource management includes the following functions

I. Manpower Planning

Manpower planning is the planning of the activities relating to the human resource of an organization. The process of manpower planning includes the following steps:
-Evaluation of the present manpower. It means what is the present strength of the manpower of the organization.
-Forecasting the future manpower requirements by taking into account the present activities and future expected activities
-Evaluation of the manpower problems and anticipate the future problems

II. Wages and Salary Administration

Timely payment of wages is a motivating factor to retaining employees for a longer period of time. Compensation packages should be fixed depending on the level of qualification, experience, skill, creativity, risk taking ability etc.

III. Job evaluation and performance appraisal

The major purpose of job evaluation is to determine the importance attached to the job in comparison to all other jobs. Job evaluation is done to determine the salary or wage structure and to provide for the payment for the job.

Job evaluation involves three steps:

-Job Analysis – It relates to the determination of the different components or tasks of a job.

-Job description- It relates to determination of duties, responsibilities risks in handling of tools, machines, operations etc.

-Job specification-It is the determination of the skill, qualification, experience, efforts etc.

Performance Appraisal includes the following aspects:

-Fixing a standard for the performance of a job or a duty

-Collection of information about the performance of the employee

-Measurement of performance and results there of

-Analysis of information relating to performance

-Interpretation of analysis

-Making comparative analysis aimed at decision making

IV. Training and development

Training is a learning process that is aimed at educating employees to increase resources in them for the purpose of achieving perfection. Training is aimed at attaining objectives and is provided for specific purposes only.

Training is an integral part of an organization and is provided to employees during the period of new appointment, promotion, change in the nature of job, change in technology, change in product, process, machines, operations, change in business policies, change in working conditions etc.

Training may be of three categories such as:

On-the job training – It is a method of training employees at the place of their work .Here trainer gives hands-on training to the employee which is supported by classroom training.

Off the job training –In case of off-the job training the trainee gets training at a place which is outside his place of work. Such type of training is provided when a new technology is to be inducted in the work place .

Vestibule training- Such type of training replicates the actual work situation at the place other than the actual work place.

Besides the above mentioned training methods there are some other types of trainings too. These include methods such as induction training, apprentice training, refresher training, special training, internship training, training for new jobs etc.

Whereas training relates to acquisition of new skills in the work environment Development relates to increase in the capacity of an individual by educational activities which brings some behavioural changes in an individual. The term Development is generally referred to peoples working in various managerial positions. Some of the methods include case study method, sensitive training, role play, project etc.It's objective is to prepare employees to a higher position.

V. Employee Administration

Employee administration relates to the maintenance of complete record of the employees working in the organization. The objective of maintaining such a database is to have up-to-date information which can be useful both from the point of view of the organisation as well as for various statutory and legal purposes. It includes maintenance of adequate personal record as well as service records. It includes the keeping the record of qualifications, experience, previous employment, health details, personal data, emerging contact members, rewards, punishment transfer, promotion etc.

The maintenance of above records facilitates the decision making process relating to promotion, transfer, retirement, retrenchment, deputation to other jobs, assignment of special duties and responsibilities and rewards etc. of an employee.

VI. Industrial Relations

An industrial relation is described as the relations between the employers, employees and their unions. It is also described as the relation among employees, employees and the government. Industrial relations aim at maintaining the peace and harmony in an organization.

Industrial relation aim at:

-Developing mutual faith and understanding among employer and employee

- Grievance redressal

- Settlement of industrial disputes

-Developing industrial democracy

-Solution of employee related problems

One of the major elements of individual relations in the settlement of disputes where the employees are represented by their unions and government is represented by the authorities of the labour and employment department. Settlement of dispute is done through bipartite, tripartite settlement and labour courts.

VII. Employee Welfare

Employee welfare is the efforts made by the employer to improve the work life of the employee. The aim of welfare provisions in an organization is to create a conducive atmosphere in the organization for the employees to perform their best. In many organisations welfare officers are appointed to look after the welfare of the employees. Welfare measures in an organization include provision for first-aid, canteen, wash room facilities, shelter, restroom, lunchroom, crèches, ESI etc.

VIII. Corporate Social Responsibility

Corporate Social responsibility refers to the relationship between the organization and public. Corporate Social Responsibility is an Organization's effort to pay back the stakeholders and public who

contributed to their growth and success. Section 135 of the Indian Companies Act,2013 specifies that every company including it's holding and subsidiary company and having either a net worth of Rs.500 crore or a turnover of not less than 1000 crores or having a net profit of not less than 5 crores must follow the provisions of section 135 of the Act. Where a Company fulfils any of these conditions the company will have to set aside 2% of the average net profits and these funds will be utilised for any or more of the below mentioned activities for the society:
-Eradication of hunger, malnutrition or poverty
-Promotion of healthcare and sanitation
-Offering educational support for enhancing vocational skills
-Encouraging gender equality
-Ensuring sustainability
-Protecting heritage
-Working for the benefit of the country's armed forces
-fostering and training for sports activities
-contributing to relief projects etc.

FINANCIAL MANAGEMENT IN SMALL BUSINESS

Proper management of finance results in profitability of any business enterprise. Hence for an entrepreneur it is important to have an understanding of finance. Some of the components of financial management include the following:

-Investment Decision:

Investment decision relate to the decisions relating to deployment of funds and it takes into account various factors .These factors include the return on investment from similar type of projects earned by existing business, internal rate of return and time value of money. Further it includes factors like breakeven point of the project, expected increase in demand in the future period and the competition, both existing and upcoming. Based on this the entrepreneur has to decide whether the funds should be invested in a particular project or not. Investment decisions are basically of two types. One is long-term investment decision also known as capital budgeting decision, which relate to investing in those assets from which revenue will be earned. On the other hand short –term investment decisions relate to procurement of current assets including purchase of raw materials and also making payments for current liabilities which relate to payment of salaries and wages. The entrepreneur should make it sure that funds procured for long-term purposes are invested in long-term assets and funds obtained for working capital purposes are utilized there.

-Financing Decisions:
Financing decision relates to the sources from which funds will be procured and what should be the cost of these funds so that the financial risk can be minimized. The sources of fund basically are of two types. One is owner's fund, which is also known as equity capital or share capital, and outsiders fund or debt fund. Funds obtained from outside sources could be either through public borrowing or bank loan which involves interest payment either annually or bi-annually basis. On the other hand dividend to be paid on equity capital need not be paid at a fixed rate or amount. So depending on the profitability of the project financing decision has to be taken.

-Dividend Decision: Dividend decisions relate to the profit of the organization. It states what percentage of the profits will be paid to owners and the shareholders and what percentage is to be retained for future expansion purposes.

-Liquidity decision-Liquidity is an important aspect of financial management. One should not have too much cash in hand because idle fund earns nothing. On the other hand inability to pay the current liability due to shortage of cash for day to day payment purposes results in loss of credibility for any enterprise.

-Proper use of surplus funds- In case of availability of excess fund these should be invested in short-term marketable and liquid securities so that excess funds do not lie idle and at the same time could be available at a short notice.

Financial Planning
Financial planning involves determination in advance of the in-

flow and outflow of finance for the organization. This requires the preparation of financial budget. Budget is an estimate or plan for any activity. For example cash budget gives an estimate of the cash receipts and payments for a particular period. Budgets could be classified into various categories .When budgets are prepared for a particular period then it could be annual budget, bi-annual budget, quarterly budget, monthly budget and daily budget etc. On the other hand it could also be prepared for various departments or activities or operations. We can classify operational budgets into various categories like Sales Budget, Purchases Budget, Production Budget, Financial Budget etc.

MARKETING MANAGEMENT

Marketing Management is concerned with the process of management of marketing programs for achieving organisational objectives. It helps in designing strategies for the purpose of creation of demand in the mind of the people and supplying goods and services to satisfy their demand.

Although demand for goods or services remains in the hands of users of the goods and the seller has very little control over it but a successful marketing management programme can help to make the customers depend on the enterprise.

Definition of Market:

In general market is understood to be the place where goods and commodities are exchanged for sale and purchase. It is a place where two parties, i.e. buyer and seller, meet to facilitate the exchange of goods and services. The market may be a tangible or physical one like a shop or a retail outlet or online market where there is no physical interaction between the seller and the buyer.

Classification of Market: Markets could be classified in a number of ways. Some of these methods of classifications are as follows:

Area wise classification: Markets can be classified according to the area of their operation. Under this category markets can be classified as Local market, regional market, national market, international market.

According to Nature of product: Markets can also be classified depending on the products traded in those markets. Under this category markets can be classified as textile market, money market, capital market, bullion market, spice market etc.

According to volume of transaction: Markets in this category can be classified as either retail markets or wholesale markets.

According to time factor : Markets under this category could be classified as daily market, weekly market, short term market, long term market etc. depending on the time period during which the market operates.

From Economics Point of view: We could categorise markets as Monopoly market, oligopoly market, perfect market, imperfect market etc. under this category.

Meaning and definition of marketing

Marketing is an activity through which exchange of ownership of goods and their considerations takes place and includes both buying and selling. Philip Kotler defines marketing as "Satisfying needs and wants through an exchange process". Marketing includes activities relating to identification of customers as well as prospective customers, ascertaining their needs and desires, creation of desires and needs, and creation of customers .It involves communicating with the customers, supply of appropriate goods and satisfaction and achievement of the goal of the enterprise through all those activities.

FUNCTIONS OF MARKETING:

-**Collection of market information and make marketing research**- This is the primary function which means before deciding about a product launch one must identify the needs, wants and demands of the consumers of the intended segment of the market to which the product is targeted. For this market research is an important tool. Market Research could either be done in-house or could be outsourced to external agencies depending on the available manpower ,time and resources.

-**Product Designing and Development**-After getting the feedback from market research team and depending on the information on research and development product design and development is done. The objective is not only to make the product cost effective but also to make the product look attractive and durable.

-Identification of the target groups- It includes identifying the segment where the product will be marketed, understanding them and studying their requirements from all possible angles to know their taste, fashion, habit, custom etc.

- Branding and Packaging:
Branding is the process of assigning a distinct name to the product so as to differentiate it from the competitive products of similar nature. If the brand is given a name it is called 'brand mane'. Examples are: NIRMA Washing Powder, Mysore Sandal Soap etc.

Packaging:
Packaging is considered as an important element of product mix. Some experts even consider it as fifth P along with product, price, promotion and physical distribution. It is the art, science and technology of preparing goods for the purpose of transport and sale. Packaging has thus two important aspects:

1. It helps in physical distribution/transportation and sale of the products.
2. It performs the functions of selecting package design and packaging material.

Benefits of Packaging

1. **Safeguarding the product**: Packaging protect the product from damage in the process of transit, storage and use.
2. **Appeal**: Packaging makes the product more attractive and appeals to the customers.
3. **Convenience:** The package should be convenient to use. It should be easy to open and close the package, it should have repetitive use value etc.
4. **Cost effectiveness**: The package should be cost-effective too.

Legal Issues to be mandated on Packaging:
There are certain regulations which must be followed in respect of

packaging of goods. Main among these is the product information given in the package known as "labelling requirements". Label is a display of written, printed or graphic matter on the package/container of the product. Labelling needs to fulfil the following statutory requirements.
1. Net weight of the package when packed.
2. Date of manufacture.
3. Date of expiry.
4. Minimum retail price including local taxes
5. Directives of use
6. Directives of storage.

Pricing Policy:
Once the design of the product is decided upon, the price of the product needs to be determined before selling it in the market. The entrepreneur has to take a decision regarding the price at what the product will be sold and how the price will be determined etc.

Meaning of Price:
Price is the money that the customers will pay to avail a product or a service.
Pricing is one of the key elements of marketing mix.
The salient features of pricing are:
-Pricing covers all marketing aspects like the goods or services, modes of payment, methods of distribution, currency etc.
-Pricing may carry with it certain benefits to customers like guarantee, free delivery, installation, free after sale servicing and so on.
-Pricing may refer to different price of a product for different customers and different prices for the same customer at different times.

Factors affecting price:
The important factors that may apply to all types of products are:
-**Product Characteristics**: It includes product lifecycle, the perishability of the product, product satisfaction etc.
-**Product Cost:** In order to optimize the product cost various costs

like fixed cost, variable cost, and incremental costs have to be taken into account.

-Objectives of the firm: The objectives set by the firm influences the price of the product. For example if the high adopts skimming objectives, the price set would be high. On the other hand, if the firm adopts the market penetration as its objectives, the prices set would be normally low.

-Competitive Situation: Competitive situation plays a part in price fixation. In a monopolistic market the entrepreneur can set a price that suits him. On the other hand if the product is novel and it will take some time for the competitors to build their position then in that case the entrepreneur may set a high introductory price. However if the product is an existing one available in the market and competition is there then in that case lower introductory price could be offered to create a customer base.

-Demand for the product: Pricing also depends on the demand for the product. If there is enough demand for the product, i.e.if demand exceeds supply then in that case the entrepreneur can set a price suitable to him, provided there is no substitute products.

-Government Regulations: At times the regulatory measures restrict the maximum price that could be set for a product. The entrepreneur must keep it in mind.

Pricing Policies / Methods

-Cost plus pricing method: Under this type of pricing method selling price is determined by adding a certain percentage of profit to the unit cost price of the product.

-Skimming Pricing: Under this method of pricing the entrepreneur sets a relatively high introductory price for a product or service which he lowers as the demand for the product or service declines.

-Penetration Pricing: This method is applicable when the entrepreneur is confident that by lowering the initial price of the product it can create new customer bases that are using the product or service of competitors. Here the price of the product is lower than similar type of products or services available in the market. It helps in creating a buzz about the product or service.

-**Market Rate Policy**: Under this method the price set for the product or service is the usual price that is applicable to similar kind of products or services.

-**Variable Price Policy:** Under this method the price of a product is not same but different at different locations or points of sale.

Market Segmentation

Market segmentation is an attempt to make the marketing strategies customers oriented. It is the activity of grouping of buyers or customers to create a segment. It could be an existing one or a new segment.

Criteria for Market Segmentation:

The following are some of the criteria for creating market segmentation

-Geographical Variables-Here the market segment is made according to geographical areas. For example eastern markets and western markets.

-Demographic Variables-Demographic variables include population variables like age, sex, marital status etc.

-Educational variables : Here the market segmentation is made as per the educational qualification. For example literate and illiterate, under graduates and graduates.

- Income variables-Here the segmentation is made by taking into account the level of income which varies across places, occupation, educational attainment etc.

-Psychological variables-It relates to the psychology of the customers. These are due to personality, lifestyle, tastes, interests etc.

Marketing Mix

Marketing Mix is centred on the 4 Ps of marketing which includes product, price, place and promotion. The business organization uses various marketing tools to foray into the desired market or the desired segment of the market to pursue its marketing objectives. In modern marketing practices a few more Ps are added to the Existing Ps to expand the possibility of attaining marketing objectives. These include People, Process and Physical Environment.

Price indicates as to how much the product is worth. This is a factor of production costs, competition, consumer demographics, supply chain, and pricing strategy.

Product refers to the item or service to be offered sale. It is a combination of performance, features, design and competition.

Place indicates where the product will be sold. This includes online marketing, retail stores or through direct selling.

Promotion refers to creating awareness amongst people regarding the product or service. It includes advertising in media, direct marketing, social media campaigns etc..

Physical environment refers to the market whether a physical storefront presence or creating it's presence felt in the minds of consumers.

Process refers to the system involved in the marketing process.

People includes the individuals supporting the product, either as service providers, marketers, or otherwise.

Problems of Marketing in Small Scale Sector
-Competition with modern sector:
There is an assumption that the goods manufactured by the small scale sector are not of high quality, thus leading to lesser acceptability and sales as compared to the large scale sector.

Lack of sales promotion:
Advertising of the products through the elaborate sales promotions methods such as through trained salesman, advertisement in print and electronic mediums is very much essential for a new as well as established product, however due to lack of resources and trained people small scale industries lack in the sale promotion.

Weak Bargaining power
Small entrepreneurs have weak bargaining power with the buyers and as a result profitability also becomes low.

Market Assessment
A small scale enterprise must first of all assess the target group

of customers to who the products or services is meant for. After having indentified the target group of customers, next the demand for the product or service is to be estimated. Demand forecasting helps the entrepreneur in this task.

There are a number of techniques available for forecasting the demand. The important methods are as follows:

A. Survey Method

This method is widely used for estimating demand of a product. Under this method, customers or dealers are surveyed in order to avail the requisite information. Basically this method is followed by using samples.

B. Statistical Method

Under this method historical data on the demand of the product are used to forecast the future trend, for example, if the relationship between the customer's income and the demand for a product is well established then regression analysis may be used to estimate the demand for the product at various levels of the consumer's income.

C. Leading Indicator Method:

Under this method some indications are taken as a future trend. For example if the Govt. gives permission to increase automobile production, it indicates that there will be an increase in the demand for automobile accessories.

CHAPTER SIX
Entrepreneurial Motivation

By now, you must have gained some idea about entrepreneur and entrepreneurship, i.e. what qualifies a person to become an entrepreneur and what he does. You might have also learnt that the entrepreneur plays a risk bearing role which is a difficult one.

Next we will be discussing certain important questions pertaining to entrepreneurship:

1. What prompts a person to choose a path which is not always rosy and chances of failure are always there.
2. What motivates people to enter into business which is often difficult?

Although the motivations for venturing into new areas and projects vary widely, the reason cited most frequently for becoming an entrepreneur is independence, i.e. not wanting to work under anyone's supervision .Various studies show that the desire to be one's own boss is what drives both male and female entrepreneurs around the world to accept all the social psychological and financial risks. Other motivating factors differ between male and female entrepreneurs and vary from country to country. Money is the second most motivational factor for starting a new venture for man, whereas job satisfaction, achievement, opportunity and money are the reasons in the ranking order for women.

Role Models and Support Systems

One of the most important factors influencing entrepreneurs in their career path is their choice of a role model. Role models can be parents, brothers, sisters, relatives or other entrepreneurs.

Role models can also serve in a supportive capacity as mentors during and after the launch of anew venture. An entrepreneur needs a strong support and advisory system in every phase of the new venture. It is most crucial during the start-up phase, as it provides information advice and guidance on matters such as organizational structure, obtaining the required financial resources and marketing.

Moral support Network

It is important for each entrepreneur to establish a moral support network of family and friends who act as a cheering squared. This cheering squad plays a critical role during the difficult and lively times that occur throughout the entrepreneurial process. Most entrepreneurs indicate that their spouses one their biggest supporters and allow them to devote the excessive amount of time necessary for the new venture.

Friends also play key role in the moral support network.

Finally relatives (Children's, parents, grandparent, aunts and uncles) can also be a strong source of support.

Professional Support Network

In addition to encouragement, an entrepreneur needs advice and counsel for establishing a new venture. This advice can be obtained from a mentor, business associates, trade associations or personal affiliations which form a part of professional support network.

Suppliers are another important component in a professional – support network. Suppliers can provide good information on nature and competition in the industry.

Trade association can help to keep the new venture competitive. Trade associations keep up with the new developers and can provide overall industry data.

Finally, personal affiliations in clubs, alumina groups of the entrepreneur can also be a valuable part of professional

Motivating Factors:

The factors that motivate an entrepreneur basically fall into the following two Categories:

(1)Internal Factors:
- a. **Desire to do something new**-This factor motivates a person to do something new instead of the traditional method of living the life. To come out of the traditional shackles and to develop some new methods and processes

and to follow that practice requires a lot of courage and strong willpower.
  b. **Educational background:** All entrepreneurs are not highly educated persons. People with variable educational background become entrepreneurs. However education gives confidence to achieve. An educated person is more acquainted with the new-age technology which is very important to be successful in the new age technological era.
  c. **Occupational background or experience** – A person having a set of skills or occupational experience is more likely to become successful than the one having no such experience. The reason behind this success is that the experienced person is more likely handle the initial teething problem in any start-up.

(2)External Factors:
a.**Government assistance and support**-Sometimes various schemes and programs of Government aids a person to become an entrepreneur. Government assistance includes providing initial financial assistance in low rate of interest, tax holiday, making various hubs for a particular type of business etc.
b.**Availability of labour and raw material** – Easy availability of labour and raw materials plays an important role in the entrepreneurial motivation process.
c.**Encouragement from big business houses** – When big business houses outsources some of their production processes to small scale industries then it gives rise to advent of more entrepreneurs. For example in case of automobile industry ancillary units develop to supply their products to big automakers.
d.**Promising demand for the product**- When the demand for a product is in the upward trend it gives rise to the creation of more entrepreneurs.
e .**Advice of business friends** -   Sometimes a person gets motivated by the words or advice of a friend who runs a business to start his own business venture.

f. Profits earned by friends in similar concerns- When a person willing to start a business venture sees that there is prospects in a particular type of business on which his friends are making money he gets motivated to run such type of business.

g. Unsound Units available at cheap price – At times some industrial units become unsound or sick .However it sometimes attracts certain other set of people who believes that the sick unit can be turned around.

CHAPTER SEVEN

Entrepreneurial Traits and Skills

It is a fact that all entrepreneurs do not become successful at the first go. Some become successful with their first venture and continue that trend throughout their life, where as others do not become that successful .Thus a question arises what are the qualities that make an entrepreneur successful. The possession of these qualities includes a certain knowledge, skill or personality profile called entrepreneurial traits which help the entrepreneurs perform better.

Meaning of entrepreneurial Trait

Competence or Trait is an underlying characteristic of an individual leading to his/her effective and superior performance in a job. A job competence is a combination of a person's underlying characteristics such as knowledge, skill, motive etc. which one uses to perform a given job well. However the existence of these underlying characteristics may or may not be known to the concerned person. These underlying characteristic that are possessed by an entrepreneur leading to his superior performance it is called entrepreneurial competencies or traits.

The entrepreneurial competencies or traits are based on the following key components:

I. Knowledge

Knowledge can be referred to as collection and retention of information in one's mind. It is essential and important for performing any job. For example when one reads a book which describes how to cook certain items then the person reading the book can understand the process of cooking, the ingredients required for cooking an item of a food properly and for how long and in what process the cooking will be done. But just by reading a book or watching a television channel does not make a person an expert cook. Similarly a person having knowledge of playing cricket could be in a position to describe as to how to play cricket but nothing more than that.

It indicates that in order to perform a job in the desired manner and in a satisfactory mode one also need to have skills to translate the knowledge into action.

II. Skill

Skill is the ability to perform a job effectively by using one's knowledge which is observable, i.e. something that one can see. Skill can be divided into two categories. One is general skill and the other one is Specific Skill. For example general skills could include leadership, ability to work with others whereas specific skills relate to the job of the individual. A skilled person can identify the sequence of events to be performed to complete his job successfully.

Thus, while the knowledge of playing cricket could be acquired by reading, discussing etc., skill can be acquired only by practice, i.e., playing on a number of occasions. This means both knowledge and skill are required to perform a task.

III. Motive

In simple terms, motive is an urge or desire to achieve one's goal. The continuous concern towards goal achievement directs a person to perform better and better. Coming back to the example of cricket playing, one's urge to become the best player directs him to practice cricket thoroughly to look out for ways and means to improving his play. Similarly if a person wants to be a best cook and earn name and fame for himself then he must have the desire for it and should apply his domain skill to get the best out of himself.

This, in order to perform any task effectively and successfully including establishing and running an industrial unit, an entrepreneur needs to possess a set of knowledge, skill and motive which could be termed together as entrepreneurial traits or competencies.

Major Entrepreneurial Traits or Competencies

We learnt in the earlier discussions that entrepreneurs must have some skills and motive to become successful entrepreneur. The following is a list of some of those competencies, the presence of which in an individual could lead to superior performance as an entrepreneur.

1. **Initiative**: The entrepreneur must be enterprising enough to initiate a business activity.
2. **Opportunity Seeker**: He must always look for an opportunity and use his resources to utilize the chance and should take appropriate actions as and when required.
3. **Persistence:** It means continuous efforts without fearing failures. The entrepreneur must make repeated efforts to overcome obstacles that arise while realizing goals.
4. **Information seeker**: To succeed in his venture the entrepreneur constantly needs information regarding demand-supply position, consumption pattern and changes if any, industrial production and exports .He must take the help of various research agencies and should consult experts to get information to help him reach the goal.
5. **Quality Conscious**: He must have a strong urge to excel and must maintain the quality of his products and services. Further in order to gain market share he should see that his product quality is better than the existing standard.
6. **Efficiency seeker**: Makes always efforts to get the task completed within minimum cost and time.
7. **Good planner**: It is the task of the entrepreneur to formulate plans that are realistic and proper and then to execute these plans rigorously to accomplish the task in hand.
8. **Problem Solver**: The entrepreneur must always try to find

out ways and means to solve the problems that comes before him and should try to tide over the difficult times.
9. **Self-Confidence**: The entrepreneur must be very high on confidence and must have the belief on his own strengths and abilities.
10. **Assertiveness**: The entrepreneur must confront any situation very boldly and should have the courage to tell directly as to what he expects from any person without offending that person.
11. **Persuasiveness:** Again this is another positive quality .The entrepreneur must be able to successfully persuade others to do what he actually wants from them..
12. **Employee's Well Wisher**: The entrepreneur must have great concern for his employees and should be caring enough for them. He must come forward to help their employees in case of need and should take necessary measures to improve the welfare of employees working in his enterprise. Better treatment of employees leads to increase in productivity of the organization.
13. **Effective Strategist**: This is again a trait which makes an entrepreneur successful. The entrepreneur must be a good strategist. He must have his action plans ready to fight competition and to gain a good market share for his products and services.

Developing Competencies or Traits

We all know that Competency or Traits result in superior performance. It is not possible for an individual to possess all the qualities or traits. However wherever required the following methods could be used to develop and sharpen the entrepreneurial competency.

1. **Competency Recognition**: The first step involved in developing a particular competence is first to understand and recognize a particular competence. Thus it should

first of all be recognized as to what competency or quality which a person should have as an entrepreneur is missing
2. **Self-Assessment**: Competency recognition can be mapped by using self-assessment method. Self assessment can be done by asking certain questions to oneself. From this it can be assessed as to where one stands with respect to a particular competence and factors can be added to make that competence more distinctive. For example at times leaders, whether political or business lack certain qualities and need some refinement in their approach, however in due course and after practice they try to bring the better out of themselves.
3. **Competence Application**: Having made the self assessment and having an understanding of the shortcoming in a particular trait, that is after knowing where one stands with respect to a particular competency; one needs to improve the same on a continuous basis in various activities.
4. **Feedback**: Thus after understanding, internalizing and practicing a particular behavior or competence, one needs to make an introspection of the same in order to sharpen and strengthen one's competency.

Various Characteristics of an Entrepreneur:

The characteristics of an entrepreneur that contribute to the success of the business enterprise is the result of his achievement motivation. The following are some of the important characteristics of an entrepreneur.

1. **Strong Mental Ability**: It consists of intelligence and creative thinking. An entrepreneur must be reasonably intelligent and should have creative thinking and must be able to engage in the analysis of various problems and situations in order to deal with them.
2. **Clarity regarding objectives**: An entrepreneur should

have a clear objective as to the exact nature of business, the nature of goods to be produced etc. Objectives for an entrepreneur need not be to earn profits only it could also be to provide quality product at the least possible price or to provide benefit to the society and to do social service.
3. **Maintaining Business Secrecy**: An entrepreneur must be able to guard his business secrets.
4. **Maintaining Good Human Relationships**: Some of the important factors contributing to the success of an entrepreneur are personal relations, consideration and tactfulness. An entrepreneur must maintain good relations with customers, employees, suppliers, creditors and the community in order to succeed in business.
5. **Good Communication Skill:**: An entrepreneur must have good communication skill and must be able to communicate effectively with customers, employees, suppliers and creditors in order to succeed in business.
6. **Technical Skill**: An entrepreneur must have a reasonable level of technical knowledge.

Entrepreneurial Skills

Entrepreneurial skills are those skills which include his ability to deal with situations, organizations and social and economic forces as they emerge from time to time. These entrepreneurial skills could be categorised as follows:

1. **Group Skills:**
   - Ability to work together –The entrepreneur should have the ability to work in a group. Working together in a group requires the ability to co-ordinate the group members and various activities. As entrepreneurship involves interacting with various groups and activities hence it's important that the entrepreneur must be able to work in group.
   - Ability to work with limited resource base- This is

very important as in case of new enterprise there will be resource crunch as production or service might not have been started in full swing and also the new enterprise must expand in order to grow. Hence the entrepreneur must have the ability to work with limited resource base.
2. **Technical Skills** –The entrepreneur must be well conversant with various digital platforms, social media etc. and must be well acquainted with the current trend in technology. Because in this digital age this is the way to grow as all business depends on digital media hence the entrepreneur should be able to use the updated technology.
3. **Business management skills:** As the entrepreneur has to manage his/her business in a co-ordinated manner hence he must be well conversant with certain basic managerial skills.
    - Planning and goal setting-The entrepreneur must set a goal both short-term and long-term relating to various activities like production, marketing etc. Proper planning aids in the goal setting process.
    - Decision making- The entrepreneur must be a good and quick decision maker. He must take instant decisions as and when required so that there is no confusion amongst the employees.
    - Human relation skill- It relates to managing people in the organization. A good human relation skill will help the entrepreneur to retain the human resources for a longer period of time which is essential from the organizational point of view.
    - Marketing- Without having the understanding of marketing skills it is not possible to be a successful businessman. Hence marketing skills should be mastered by the entrepreneur and effective marketing strategy must be designed.
    - Finance-Financial skills relate to the sources from

which the finance is to be obtained and how to utilize the financial resources. This is though a basic skill but a very important skill.
4. **Individual skills** – Individual skills are concerned with the particular skills which the entrepreneur as a person possess. However it is observed that as entrepreneurs possess one or more of the following individual skills.
   - They are disciplined
   - Risk taker –They prefer to take risks. Some take outright risks whereas others take calculated risks.
   - Innovative –They are innovative in the way they think and act.
   - Visionary leader –They are visionary leaders and motivate others through their leadership qualities.
   - Ability to manage change- They have the ability to manage changes in the circumstances and the environment.
5. **Enterprise skills**-The skills include
   - Identifying value creating processes and capabilities that leads to either product differentiations or cost minimization or both
   - Market sensing skill which means changing the product or service characteristics depending on the needs of the market
   - Creating or setting new direction or vision for the organization, and
   - Learn to take risks as and when required without putting too many things at risk.
6. **Behavioural skills**-It includes
   - Motivation- Motivating fellow employees to get the best out of them and to achieve goals in the process
   - Judgmental ability – Ability to judge the importance of the matter and taking instant decisions
   - Self Management –The entrepreneur must learn how to manage his times and to find more time for important assignments.

7. **Communication skills-** Communication skill include the following
   - Ability to identify an opportunity to communicate – People in leadership position must identify opportunity to communicate with employees and associates. During various celebrations the leaders should mingle with employees which create fellow feeling among employees.
   - Putting the intelligence into words-It is important to express the positive feelings and appreciation both in words and in incentives to the employees working hard for the organization.
   - Emphasize on the issue – While dealing with employees relating to any issue the entrepreneur must emphasize on the incident and the resulting issue. No employee should be of the opinion that the authority has any personal ill feeling for him.
8. **Listening Skills**-Listening skills include the following
   - Listen without interruption of any thoughts –Listening skill is one of the most important skill. By listening attentively it creates an effect in the mind of the aggrieved person that the higher authority is genuinely interested to sort out issues if any.
   - Pay attention to others- While listening to employees, associates or vendor one should pay attention. If the entrepreneur behaves as if he is not interested it does not create a good impression in the mind of the other person.
9. **Soft skills**

The following skills are also part of the skill set that the entrepreneurs is supposed to possess:
   - Good knowledge of English and of the local language of the place where the entrepreneur generally works or is expected to work or start his entrepreneurial venture.
   - Using one's knowledge effectively and diligently is

equally important for any entrepreneur.
- Clarity in expressions is essential because sometimes improper expressions and inappropriate body language creates problem without any such intention on the part of the entrepreneur.

CHAPTER EIGHT

Environmental Dynamics and Changes

Entrepreneurial environment refers to the various facets within which many small, medium and large enterprises operate. The various factors that contribute to entrepreneurship are varied and many. However, such factors can be broadly classified into the following in broad Categories:
(1) Social Environment
(2) Economic Environment
(3) Cultural Environment
(4) Facilitating Environment
(5) Compelling Environment
(6) Psychological Environment
(7) External Environment

A. Social Environment: Social factors strongly affect entrepreneurial development. Social factors include the following:

-Attitude of people towards work-It is very important for the growth of entrepreneurship. If the peoples in an area or country do not have the attitude for hard work then entrepreneurship cannot thrive in that area. Large Multinational Corporations prefer to set up industries and manufacturing units in Asian Countries like because peoples in Asian Countries are hard working.

-Attitude of people towards wealth – If people don't want to earn money and create wealth for themselves and for the economy then entrepreneurship cannot thrive. If entrepreneurship has to grow then people must have positive attitude towards wealth.

-Intelligence and education level of people- Entrepreneurial growth is possible when the level of education and intelligence of the people in a region is high. Entrepreneurial activity in a country or region increases when the intelligence and the education level of people increases. Educated people have more understanding of the system, business environment and government machinery and could exert proper control over their business venture.

B. Economic Environment: Economic Environment refers to those economic factors which have a bearing on the entrepreneurship. Some of these factors are as follows:

(i) **Economic system**: Economic system of a country has a bearing on the entrepreneurial activities. Economies around the world can be divided into three basic categories. These are Socialist Economy, Capitalist Economy and Mixed Economy. Entrepreneurship is encouraged in capitalist economy and mixed economy. However in socialist economy though scope is there, it is limited.

(ii) **Industrial policies**: Govt. from time to time declares industrial policy. Industrial policies define the category of Industries like medium, small and micro industries and a tax incentive that they could avail. It also expresses the priority area of the Government.

(iii) **Financial policies**: Financial policies of the Govt. include taxation policy and monetary policy. Through monetary policy Govt. regulates the availability of money in the economy. Similarly taxation policy determines the tax structure and tax incentives available to Business.

(iv) **Price and Distribution control**: If Govt. imposes Price control or distribution control or both on any Goods or Services then in that case the entrepreneur cannot increase the price of that product or service without the permission of the Govt. Such type of policy may not encourage an industry to grow.

C. Cultural Environment:

Culture Environment consists of values and behaviour acceptable within the society. It includes democracy, autocracy, socialist, economy etc. Entrepreneurship is easy and gets encouragement in democratic environment because of the liberal attitude of people and that of Govt. However this is not the case in case of autocratic and socialist economic environment

D. Facilitating Environment

Entrepreneurs need to get constant motivation and encouragement to carry on their present as well as future endeavours. Parents, mentors and friends act as facilitators to motivate the entrepreneurs.

E. Compelling Environment –There are certain compelling environments which encourage individuals to become an entrepreneur.

(i) **Excess funds lying idle**-It can encourage one to become entrepreneur. This happens when a person gets large sum of money either as planned or unplanned. This could arise during the time of retirement, Voluntary retirement from job, winning a lottery, gains from speculation and funds from insurance claim or settlement.

(ii) **Technical knowledge**: When a person has a vast technical knowledge he may decide to go for his own enterprise instead of working for an employer.

(iii) **Manufacturing experience**: Similarly a person having years of manufacturing experience may decide to start his own manufacturing set-up and earning higher amount of income instead of working for any industry at a lower pay packet.

F. Business experience :Like manufacturing experience a person working in a business house or a trading concern for a number of years and closely observing the business dealings learns the tricks of business. So later on he may decide to work for himself and become his own boss instead of working for others.

G. Psychological Environment: Sometimes psychological environment helps individuals to become entrepreneurs. Individuals get psychologically motivated to become entrepreneurs when they prefer personal responsibility for decisions, are moderate risk takers and possess interest in concrete knowledge of results and decisions.

H. External Environment: External environment plays a vital role in making the entrepreneurial venture a successful one. It includes the following aspects:

(i) **Financial assistance from institutional sources**: In order to convert an idea into a reality funds are required. So when an entrepreneur gets financial assistance from financial institutions or Banks it helps him to realize his dreams and convert his dreams into reality.

(ii) **Accommodation in Industrial Estate** – When an entrepreneur gets a proper place to carry on his manufacturing activities or service provisions in designated Industrial Estates he can carry his activities with a lot of confidence.

(iii) **Attitude of Government** – It is the most important one as ultimately it is the Govt. Policy which encourages entrepreneurs. Providing good infrastructure, building and framing a proper fiscal policy, monetary policy, industrial policy and budgetary policy goes a long way in encouraging entrepreneurs.

(iv) **Encouragement from large business** : Entrepreneurs gets encouragement when large industries helps them in setting up ancillary industries and these industries in the small-scale sector supply their finished products as inputs for large industries.

(v) **Machinery on hire-purchase** : When machineries are available on hire-purchase scheme to be used by industries in easier and flexible term it gives rise to more industries.

(vi) **Market** : Availability of good buyer's market helps the entrepreneur to become confident in selling his products and expansion and growth of his business.

Ideas vs. Money in commencing New Venture

Having ideas alone is not sufficient to create an enterprise. It will require money to convert ideas into activities. Similarly simply having money shall not create enterprise. It will require ideas to create enterprise. Thus one needs both money and ideas to run an enterprise.

Ideas must be innovative and should be capable of being transformed into finished products. It should also be supported by a strong marketing plans right vision. An analytical vision shall be helpful to make distinction between right and wrong ideas.Futher through ideas one must visualize the demand of the product for a longer period of time. Thus vision should be for a longer period of time.

However we cannot ignore the fund requirement for any new project. It is a must for any enterprise and for a new enterprise the requirement is still more as the product is yet to find a place in the market and hence it takes time to get money through sales. The sources of funds may vary from one entrepreneur to the other but the basic sources of funds include funds from personal savings, loans and advances from banks and financial institution etc. Obtaining long-term credit for infrastructural requirement including land, building, plant and machineries etc. shall be helpful for the enterprise.

Entrepreneurial Success and Failure Factors

Success of an enterprise may be due to many reasons. At times an entrepreneur feels helpless in certain situations. The factors requisite for the success of an enterprise and an entrepreneur could broadly be grouped into two categories. (i) Internal reasons and (ii) External reasons

   (i) **Internal Factors**

      (a) Efficient management plays an important role in the success of an enterprise.

      (b) Quality of goods and services-If the quality of goods and services provided by the entrepreneur are of good quality people will prefer to buy these products again and again and it will result in the growth of the enterprise.

      (c) Good reputation of the business and its products- Reputation of the company and its products play a vital role. People go for those products which can give a good feeling for being associated with that product.

      (d) Good reputation of the entrepreneur –Reputation of the entrepreneur helps in selling of the product and providing good profit to the organization.

      (e) Low cost of production –Lower the cost of production

higher is the flexibility in setting price for the product and more resultant profit.

(f) Effective marketing and selling network helps in the success of a product or service.

(g) Proper financial management includes getting funds in proper time, obtaining funds at a lower rate of interest and proper management of short-term funds.

(h) Dedicated manpower –Having a dedicated manpower is a boon for any organization and for any entrepreneur.

(i) Appropriate technology- Technology adopted should be as per the market requirement and it should be easy to operate and serviceable.

(j) Timely updating of products and technology

(ii) External Factors

(a) Availability of appropriate raw materials at affordable price is a must for any organization to survive. At times organizations become sick because of lack of availability of raw materials

(b) Availability of quality manpower-Unavailability of quality manpower can play a negative impact on the fortune of the Organization.

(c) Increase in demand- Where there is an increased demand for the products and services of any organization it results in increase in sales and as a result more profits.

(d) Suitable Govt. policies- Suitable Govt.policies in the form of higher amount of subsidies, tax-rebate, and tax holiday can help in making an entrepreneur successful.

(e) Low level of competition-When the level of Competition is low it results in higher sales and consequently results in more revenue.

(f) Opening of new markets- When some new markets for products and services open up which was earlier not accessible to the entrepreneur it results in profitability of the entrepreneur.

Similarly failure may also be grouped into the categories: (i) Internal reasons and (ii) External Reasons which are as follows

(i) **Internal Reasons for Failure**
   a) Ineffective management
   b) Obsolete technology
   c) Poor financial management
   d) Ineffective sales and marketing
   e) Poor quality of products and services
   f) Higher cost of production
   g) Poor quality of inputs
   h) Poor industrial relations
   i) Low quality of HR
   j) Improper leadership

(iii) **External Reasons for Failure**
   (a) Shortage of raw material
   (b) Shortage of power
   (c) Shortage of finance
   (d) Change in technology
   (e) Change in taste, fashion etc.
   (f) Higher level of competition
   (g) Reduction in demand
   (h) Increase in supply
   (i) Change in Govt. policies
   (j) Availability of better substitute and alternatives natural causes.

CHAPTER NINE

Business Plan

The business plan is a written document prepared by the entrepreneur that describes all the relevant external and internal elements involved in starting a new venture. It is an integration of various functional plans such as marketing, finance, manufacturing and human resources. It also addresses both short term and long term decision making areas for the first three years of operation. Banks, Financial Institutions, Potential investors, suppliers and customers will request or require a business plan.

A well written Business Plan is the key to the Success of an Organization. There are a number of reasons for which a Business may succeed or fail. Some of the reasons for which a Business failure takes place could be as follows:

1. Poor Customer Service- Customers play a very important role in the success story of any entrepreneur. Howevever it is not enough if your advertisement draws the customers into your showroom or to your website. Pre sales service as well as Post sales service play a very important role. Customers should feel that they are important to the Organization.

2. Poor Logistics and Cost Management – Poor logistics and Cost Management is another area which needs detailed attention. One must obtain the right inputs for production at right price and must take care of the fact that there is no stoppage of work due to non availability of raw materials.

3. Inadequate Profit.

However the most important reason for the failure of a Business is the lack of a well prepared Business Plan. A well written and a well executed Business Plan goes a long way in the Success of a Business.

Who should write the Business Plan- The business plan should be prepared by the entrepreneur. However since it needs knowledge in the various fields like Law and Business Management and Project Management hence the entrepreneur may consult with the lawyers, accountants, marketing consultants and engineers for the preparation of his plan.

Scope of this plan

The business plan may be read by potential employees, potential investors, bankers, venture capitalists, suppliers, customers, advisors, and consultants. The business plan is important to these people because:

-It helps them to determine the viability of the venture in a designated market.

-It provides guidance to the entrepreneur in organizing his or her planned activities.

-It serves as an important tool in helping to obtain finance.

What is a Business Plan?

Business plan is the description of various activities to be performed by an entrepreneur in future for the purpose of establishment of an enterprise. This includes the important decisions to be made by the entrepreneur relating to the following.

1. What are the various product/s and service/s to be to be offered by the Company?

It relates to the decision regarding the types of products and services to be offered by the entrepreneur for which he wants to set up the business.

2. What is the Vision and Mission of the Organization?

Vision and Mission statements play a very crucial role in expressing the intent and the seriousness of the Entrepreneur. Basically vision is the strategic intent of the entrepreneur and it relates to his aspiration and mental perception relating to his Business in the future period. Whereas Vision relates to a future period and gives a glimpse of the future state of the Organization Mission statement is a statement relating to the purpose of existence of the Organization.

3. What are the Goals and Objectives?

Goals represent the future attainments through concrete efforts made by the organization as a whole. It could include both financial and non financial goals. For example financial goal could include attaining 20% return on investment in next five years. Similarly non financial goal may be achieving 80% capacity utilization in next two years of time. Objectives are the ends to attain these goals. Objectives help the organization to pursue it's vision and Mission.

4. Define the Unique Selling Proposition of your Product or Service

It relates to the specific qualities of your product and service and it explains how the product or service is different from that of the other Competitors. It explains why amongst so many similar typed products or services the customer will chose your product or service and not that of your competitors.

5. Where to Market and How to Market.

It means what is the scope of the product. Whether it will be sold in the local market, foreign market, national market, international market etc.It means whether it will be sold through direct marketing, online marketing, tying up with online platform or should it be sold through dealer,distributor network etc.

6. How much money shall be invested?

It is very important to know about the cost of the project. Because based on the cost of the project the funds have to be arranged. Based on this information the capital structure of the firm will be finalised.

7. How much profit will be earned?

Again it is important. Because entrepreneur does some activity to make gain. If the profit is not sufficient to pay for financial charges then it will be difficult to run the business. Hence profit is very important component of Business Plan

8. When to start the project?

Again another important component of any Business Plan. For example if you want to manufacture an woollen garment then the project should be started in such a time that it will be completed before the arrival of winter so that production can begin immediately during winter when the demand for the product is peek.

9. Marketing and Sales Plan

This plan is very important for the success of a product and services. A number of organizations have failed in the market place because of the incorrect study of the market. The entrepreneur must finalize the market segment and the target customer.

Information Needs

Before committing time and energy in preparing a business plan, the entrepreneur must have a quick feasibility study of the business concept to see whether there are any possible barriers to success. The information should focus on the aspects of marketing, finance and production.

Before beginning the feasibility study, the entrepreneur should clearly define the goals and the objectives of the venture. There goals help to define what needs to be done and how it will be accomplished. These goals and objectives also provide framework for the business plan, marketing plan and financial plan

Component of Business plan

Industry Analysis- In addition to the market analysis and designing a suitable market, price and customer base an entrepreneur must be well aware about the industry in which he/she intend to continue his/her Business.

Industry consists of a group of Companies which are related based on similar kind of products or services manufactured by them or service provided by them. For example when we say automobile industry it includes all the companies operating in the automobile sector. Industry Analysis helps in understanding the attractiveness of the Industry. Through Industry analysis we can have a broad mapping of the various components that makes an industry either attractive or unattractive to invest. We can gauge the industry from the point of view of buyers, suppliers, new entrants, substitute products and existing participants in the industry.

Thus we can make an analysis of the industry by considering five core factors and can take a decision whether it will be advisable to do a business or not. The first factor that is to be taken into account is the bargaining power of the buyers. If in an industry buyers have a very strong bargaining power which means they can demand to make the prices of the goods and services lower, then that industry cannot be termed attractive. The absence of buyers bargaining power makes the industry attractive, which means the seller can set the prices which suits him to earn a desired amount of profit. The industry in which the sellers are more and the buyers have plenty of options then in such industry the buyers bargaining power is high. Such type of situation occurs in cases where the products are standardized and undifferentiated. In order to avoid such type of situation one may follow the strategy of product differentiation. For example instead of selling a health drink product common to all age groups it could be for working women or for children and may contain added vitamins and minerals.

Similarly if the suppliers of raw materials and components do have the bargaining power then in that case the input price can go up which means the profit will be lowered. The absence of suppliers bargaining power is good for the entrepreneur. Such situation occurs when the numbers of suppliers are less as compared to buyers and there are no other substitute inputs. This will make the industry unattractive to invest.

Similarly the absence of rivalry among competitors is a boon for the entrepreneur whereas if the rivalry is high then it will act as a deterrent. The extent of rivalry among competitors in an Industry affects the competition within that Industry. When the rivalry is weak it will lead to lesser competition and when the rivalry is high the level of competition is higher .

Again one must also look at the substitute products available in the market. Lesser the number of substitute products available in the market better it is for the entrepreneur. The easy availability of substitute products makes an industry less attractive. For example in case of the increase in the price of tea people may substitute it with coffee. Those Industries which have no close substitutes are more attractive than those which have one or more of such substitutes. Thus firms in an Industry having no close substitutes can charge a higher price and earn better returns

Finally the threat of new entrants also plays a vital role in deciding about the attractiveness of the Industry. The industry in which the profitability is high is bound to attract new entrants to the Business. The entry of new entrants to the Business depends on the presence or absence of any barriers to such entry. Barriers to entry could be in the form of Product differentiation, proprietory product technology, favourable location of the Business, easier access to raw materials,economies of scale etc.

Competitor Analysis: The objective of competitor analysis is to define not only who your competitor is but also to have an understanding of who could be potential competitor in future. This will help to face the competition in the market place. A Competitor Analysis is needed to answer the following questions

- With whom should we fight in the Industry and in what sequence
- What is the meaning of the competitor's strategic move and how seriously should we take it.

The entrepreneur must have complete details relating to his competitors. Further all the companies in the industry should not be considered as competitors. For example in the automobile Industry a two-wheeler manufacturer in a strict sense is not a competitor for a four wheeler manufacturer. However in future he may have a plan to expand his product line. Similarly even if the entrepreneur is the business of manufacturing of two wheelers then all the two-wheeler manufacturers will not be considered as competitors. For example if a two wheeler manufacturer is manufacturing a sports bike or a lifestyle bike then his product should not be considered with the manufacturer of an utility or commuter bike. Similarly the scooter manufacturer should not consider a motorcycle manufacturer as his competitor. Similarly a fast-food restaurant should not consider a lifestyle restaurant as its Competitor. Hence it is very important to make a proper competitor analysis after making a proper selection of the Competitor.

Marketing plan:

Marketing plan is designed to provide answers to three basic questions:

-Where have we been?

It It includes the organization's Strengths and weakness, background of the competition, opportunities and threats in the market place etc.

-Where do we want to go in the short run?

The entrepreneur has to ask himself about his short-run goal. The answer may vary from establishing in the market to providing a product through cost effectiveness and cost leadership.

-How to get there?

The answer to this will be the type of strategy the entrepreneur will plan to attain the objectives.It could be either through cost leadership to product differentiation or could be a combination of both.

Characteristics of Marketing Plan

(1) It should provide a strategy for accomplishing the company mission or goal.
(2) It should be based on facts and valid assumptions.
(3) An appropriate organization must be designed to implement the marketing plan
(4) It should be short and simple to understand
(5) It should specify performance criteria that will be motivated and controlled.
(6) To become successful the plan should be flexible.
(7) It should provide for continuity so that each annual marketing plan can build on it.

While making a marketing plan it is not enough if one concentrates only on his or her product rather he should find out the number of competitors the Business will have to encounter in the market place. In addition to considering the strength and weakness of his own product the competitor must take a note of the strengths and weaknesses of the product or service offered by the competitors.

At this point it is important to consider the problems faced by the costumers and what additional services the customer wants over that of the competitor and how to address that situation. The entrepreneur must put himself in the position of the customer to understand his point of view.

At this point the entrepreneur must find out the demand for his goods and services. And he should make it sure that the demand for the product is more than the supply for that product or service. Sometimes though the product supplies are more than the demand the entrepreneur can create a demand for his product by providing some additional features like better quality products, free home delivery and/or providing heavy discounts.

Situation Analysis

At this point the following questions may be answered

What is the Background of the venture?

The answer to this question gives the information regarding the objective of undertaking this particular venture. What is the viability of this project and why the entrepreneur thinks that it will succeed in future?

Strengths and weakness of the venture- The areas of strength and weakness are discussed here. What the uniqueness of this project is as compared to similar other projects and what are the weak points that should be addressed?

5. Market opportunities and threat- At this point the entrepreneur has to identify the future opportunity that the market holds for his products in future and what will be or can be taken as a threat for the future.

The organizational plan
It consists of the following steps:
(1) **Developing the management team**- At this point a management team has to be defined who will be responsible for overall activities of the Organization. It could consist of only the entrepreneur or a team consisting of his close confidents.
(2) **Finalizing the legal forms of Business**. The entrepreneur has to decide about the legal form of the business. He has to take a decision regarding whether the form of organization will be of proprietorship, partnership or limited liability type of company.
(3) **Liability of owners**- The plan must include the liability of Owners. It must give information whether the liability of the owners are limited to the extent of the value of shares or there is any additional form of guarantee in addition to the paid-up value of the shares.
(4) **Costs of starting a Business**- The Business plan must state amount required to start a Business. This information should be given in advance so that funds could be arranged accordingly.
(5) **Capital requirement and Mode of financing** – In addition to the information of the cost of starting a Business it is also necessary to provide information regarding total capital re-

quirement and what will be the mode of financing. Mode of financing means how much money will be provided by the promoters, how much will be procured through debt and bank loan.

The financial Plan

(1) **Operating and capital Budget**- The operating budget and capital budget has to be prepared which is part of the financial plan. It is a forecast of the expected revenues and expenses of the future period. Capital budget is the forecast of the expected incomes and investments in a project. These investments are made to earn revenues.

(2) **Proforma Income statement**: This statement shows the incomes earned and expenditures incurred during a period. If incomes during a period are more than the expenditure then the resultant figure is profit. If expenditures during the period is more than the incomes of the period then it results in loss.

(3) **Proforma cash flow statement**: Cashflow statement explains the actual inflow and outflow of cash from operating, financing and investing activities during a period. It does not include any fictitious items and portrays the actual figure of cash outflows and inflows.

(4) **Proforma Balance Sheet:** Proforma Balance Sheet depicts the asset and liabilities of the business on a particular date. It explains what the firm owns through fixed assets and current assets and shows what the firm owes to outsiders and what are the funds that the owners have invested in the business.

(5) **Break even Analysis**: Break Even point is the figure or number at which point of production the firm does not earn any profit. Any number of units produced beyond this point will result in a profit for the business where as any number of production below this unit will result in a loss for the Business .Hence the figure should be a lower one in order to make the business more viable. The following formula could be used for calculating Break-Even Point.

Determining The Bank Ability of The Project

Project report or business plan prepared by an entrepreneur has to be submitted to different agencies for different purposes like granting of registration, issue of license, getting clearance, getting no objection certificate, getting assurance of finance etc. Simply submitting the project report does not guarantee the license or certificate etc. The project report should be able to answer the questions the evaluator wants to know.

The figures mentioned in the report should be realistic and should be based on some logic which has to be mentioned in the project report. In short the project report should be able to project a rosy picture of the project.

Evaluation of a project report is usually based on:

(1) **Technical Appraisal** –Technical Appraisal is to understand whether the project is sound with respect to different parameters such as technology, size of plant and scale of operation, plant layout and factory building, capacity of the plant, availability of raw material, location and manpower availability etc. The purpose of technical analysis is to ensure that all the inputs required to set up the project are available.

(2) **Financial Appraisal**- The financial appraisal include financing options available to the entrepreneur, it's cost and the repayment schedule. It also includes debt-servicing schedule, working capital schedule, and schedule of cash flow from operations. Here the projections are made for the price of the product, the cost of various resources required for manufacturing goods and capacity utilization. Finally all these assumptions and schedules are translated into financial statements which include projected income statement, projected balance sheet and projected cash flow statement.

(3) **Market Appraisal**-It gives a comprehensive account of the market opportunity as well as of the marketing strategy appropriate for converting the opportunity into reality. Marketing strategy could consist of a number of components like

product quality ,price, design, distribution channels, packaging etc. Market analysis should cover the following major aspects:

    i. Analysis of Market opportunity
    ii. Planning the process of Marketing the product
    iii. Organization of the Marketing process, and
    iv. Control of the implementation of the Marketing Plan

(4) **Promoter Appraisal**- It includes the background of the promoters, their financial ability, projects and businesses handled by them earlier etc.

(5) **Social Appraisal**- The social appraisal of a project is an appraisal where projects are analyzed from the perspective of society as a whole.

(6) **Environmental Appraisal** –It is the analysis of the expected changes from the implementation of the project in the socio-economic and bio-physical factors of the environment.

CHAPTER TEN

Creating an Identity for the Business

It is very important to give an identity to your Business. It should have its unique identity which should separate it from similar type business around your area and should have its unique purpose. The following are some of the steps needed to create an Identity for the Business.

I. Name of the Business

Giving a name to your Business is the first step in the preparation of a Business Plan. It should be unique and people should identify a Business with its name as it is the first thing that a customer faces. To find a name and to finalize a name requires some time. You could talk to your friends, business associates, family members, peers, teachers and other peoples to get some idea regarding this. There are various websites to help you to finalize a name. Please make sure that the name of your Business is a unique one and no other business is registered with the same name. In order to find out whether the proposed name of your Business is unique and is not registered and used by any other business one should look for the availability of name by applying for the same. In India the registration of name could be done online by logging into the website of the Ministry of Corporate Affairs.

While applying for name one should take care of the following aspects.

1. Ensure that the proposed name of the Company does not resemble the name of another company which is registered and also must make sure that it does not violate the provisions of emblems and names (Prevention of Improper Use Act, 1950).

2. Since one cannot be sure about the availability of the name hence it is advisable to mention more than one name in the order of preference. The maximum number of names that could be included in the application may go up to six in number.

3. One should take care of the fact that the name is unique and appropriate for the kind of Business it is intended for.

4. One should not use a name which is illegal, misleading or offensive of the law of the country.

II. Details of the Promoters and Business owners

The Business plan should contain the details regarding the Promoters (Business owners). It should mention details regarding their business background if any, their educational background, their financial background etc.

III. Registered address of the Business and Contact Details:

Every Business must mention the address of the registered office of the Business. The registered address is that address to which all the communications to the Company will be adressed. Any communication including the communication by the Govt., local or statutory authorities will be dispatched to this address. In addition e-mail address and contact numbers should also be mentioned. As in today's time electronic communications through e-mail is an accepted mode of communication hence it is very important that the Business must have a proper and authentic e-mail address to which communications should be sent. Further the Business should have its own website. As today's generation is computer savvy and the use of Smart phones is prevalent hence a well designed website goes a long way in promoting the Business and taking the reach of the Business to a larger audience.

IV. Legal Status and the type of Business.

It is very important to take a decision regarding the form of the Business organization with which the business intends to register. There are various forms of Organization with which a start –up Business can register itself some of which are as follows:

>   1. Limited Liability Partnership-Limited Liability Partner-

ship (LLP) is a form of registered organization which has the flexibility of a partnership form of organization and can have all the advantages of an incorporated Company including the benefits of limited liability of a Company. Further it doesn't have the disadvantages of a Partnership agreement. In case of Partnership organizations a partner is responsible for the negligence of other partners whereas in case of Limited Liability Partnership the liability of the Partners is Limited. The LLP is a separate legal entity and the liability of the partners is limited to the extent to which they have agreed to contribute to the LLP.

2. One Person Company-The Concept of One Person Company (OPC) was introduced in the Companies Act, 2013.One Person Company can be incorporated with one person as a director and is an alternative to the sole proprietorship form of Business Organization. However the turnover of such companies should not have exceeded Rs.2 Crores in any of the previous three years and the paid –up capital of the Company should not be in excess of Rs.50 lakhs.OPC is a separate legal entity and it's liability is limited. Another advantage of OPC is that it has the advantage of getting loans based on its cash flow and collateral security.

3. Private Limited Company-This becomes a suitable form of Business Organization where the number of members are more than one. Start-ups and businesses which have higher aspirations can register in such form of organization. As per the Companies Act,2013 any company having a minimum paid up capital as may be prescribed and which by its articles

(i) Restricts the rights to transfer its shares
(ii) Restricts the maximum number of members to two Hundred, except in case of One Person Company, and
(iii) Prohibits any invitation to the public to subscribe for any securities of the Company

Will be termed as a Private Limited Company.

4. **Registered Partnership Firm-** Registered Partnership firm is a form of Business organization in which the partnership deed is registered with the registrar in order to avail the benefits of partnership.

CHAPTER ELEVEN
Define Your Business

It is very important for the entrepreneur to define the Business. The entrepreneur can make a statement of the business by clearly defining the vision, mission, goals and objectives of the Business. Further he needs to make a SWOT analysis of the Business to have an understanding of the strengths, weaknesses, opportunities and threats of the Business.

I. Write a Vision Statement

The vision of an organization refers to the broad category of long-term intentions that the organization wishes to pursue. It is broad, inclusive and futuristic. A vision is something that a firm or a person aspires to be in future. For example the dream of a management graduate may be to become a general manager in some concern or in a MNC. Some others may dream to own their successful business ventures. A firm may also dream in a similar way by the persons owning the firm.

Vision is a mental image of the future state of an organization. All the visions of an organization may or may not be achievable in the long term. However it provides the direction and energy to work towards it.

A vision to be ideal should be:
- Broad, all inclusive and forward thinking
- Mental image of the future state of the Organization
- A dream that is shared across the entire organization

II. Write a Mission Statement

The mission statement makes the vision statement attainable. A well planned mission statement defines the fundamental, unique purpose that sets a company apart from other firms of its type and identifies the scope of the company's operations in terms of products and services offered and markets served. Managers in large organizations may find it difficult to relate to broad vision statements to the organizational intent. In order to make it more clearly a mission statement is used.

A mission statement classifies the following aspects of an organization.

    (a) The reason of existence of the organization.
    (b) How the organization is different from others and
    (c) The basic beliefs, values and philosophy of the organization.

III. Define the Goals and Objectives of the Business

Goals give the idea about what the Organisation hopes to accomplish in a future period of time. They represent a future state or an outcome of the effort put in now.

Objectives are the ends that state specifically how the goals shall be achieved. They are concrete and specific in contrast to goals which are generalised.

Vision and Mission statement of a Technical Institution

VISION

To serve our nation by becoming a recognized hub of academic excellence focused on the students' career and workforce development through partnership with the industries and the communities.

MISSION

To provide quality technical education for employment, workforce development by partnering with the industries in particular and communities in general.

Vision Statement of a Theme Park

-To passionately promote peace, love and oneness through educational and inspirational activities, thrilling rides and entertaining games.

-To foster positive mental and physical Development and the renewing of mind in a relaxed environment.

Mission Statement of a Theme Park

To Create a Peaceful, friendly and quality environment to foster love, family, unity and friendship through recreation, leisure and entertainment for the total well-being of individuals and families.

Prepare a SWOT Analysis: A SWOT Analysis is prepared to make an analysis of the strengths and weaknesses of the Organization. Further it takes into account the opportunities and threats that an organization will have to encounter from various angles.

Generally Strength and Weakness relate to the internal environment of the organization whereas Opportunities and threats relate to the external environment.

An Organization's strength could relate to some of the below mentioned factors:

-Favourable Location

-Reliable Manpower

- Adequate Financial Resources

- Easy availability of Raw Material

Similarly weaknesses could relate to some of the following areas:

- Unfavourable Location
- Higher cost of Raw Material
- High Labour Cost
- Uneven Cash flow

Various opportunities could be as follows:

- Availability of purchasing power due to good monsoon
- Low Cost of Technology
- Availability of Newer Markets

Similarly threats could be as follows

- Unfavourable Business scenario

- Change in Lifestyle
- Higher Taxation etc

CHAPTER TWELVE
Defining the Market and Analysing Competitors

In general market is understood to be the place where goods and commodities are exchanged for sale and purchase. It is a place where two parties, i.e. buyer and seller, meet to facilitate the exchange of goods and services. The market may be a tangible or physical one like a shop or a retail outlet or online market where there is no physical interaction between the seller and the buyer.

Classification of Market: Markets could be classified in a number of ways. Some of these methods of classifications are as follows:

Area wise classification: Markets can be classified according to the area of their operation. Under this category markets can be classified as Local market, regional market, national market, international market.

According to Nature of product: Markets can also be classified depending on the products traded in those markets. Under this category markets can be classified as textile market, money market, capital market, bullion market, spice market etc.

According to volume of transaction: Markets in this category can be classified as either retail markets or wholesale markets.

According to time factor : Markets under this category could be classified as daily market, weekly market, short term market, long term market etc.depending on the time period during which the market operates.

From Economics Point of view: We could categorise markets as Monopoly market, oligopoly market, perfect market, imperfect market etc. under this category.

The entrepreneur has to take a decision regarding the market in which he/she want to sell his/her products. For example let's say the entrepreneur want to deal with the production and sale of garments. So in this case he/she has to decide who will be her target customer. Target customers could be classified as men in general, women in general, children, only boys, only girls, young women, women above the age of 40, men above 40, senior citizens.etc.

Let's suppose that the entrepreneur decides that his target customers will be women of all age groups. Once the entrepreneur takes a decision that the target customers will be women consisting of all age groups next step will be pricing. Pricing will depend on the target customers group and the market again. For example the entrepreneur will have to decide whether he want to sell his products to higher income customer group, middle income customer group, lower income customer group. Further he will have to decide whether he want to sell his products in the local market, national market, international market, foreign market etc. Pricing will vary depending on type of customer and the type of market. Next question comes regarding branding. If the product is not meant for mass market then a careful branding of the product will go a long way in increasing the value of the product. In addition to pricing the entrepreneur must also design a suitable packing of the product. It is very important because sometimes a product may be judged based on the packing of the product.

Once the target customer group and the pricing policy is decided upon the next step that has to be given focus is the place of sale or the mode of sale. For example here the decision will be regarding whether to sale a product online or offline. If online then the decision will be whether it it will be through our own website and exclusive app or whether it will be in association with other online sellers or whether it would include both. Similarly if the product is to be sold in offline through retail stores then what will be the strategy? And how much profit will be earned in this process?

Again awareness regarding your product and service plays a very important role in the success of a product. Here also the advertising strategy plays a vital role. Here the decision will revolve around whether the entrepreneur will go for an initial heavy spending on advertising as it is required during the initial introduction phase of a product or whether the advertisements will be done during festive seasons.

All these steps have to be well planned in advance before introduction of a product in a market.

Pricing Policy:

Once the design of the product is decided upon, the price of the product needs to be determined before selling it in the market. The entrepreneur has to take a decision regarding the price at what the product will be sold and how the price will be determined etc.

Pricing Policies / Methods

-Cost plus pricing method: Under this type of pricing method selling price is determined by adding a certain percentage of profit to the unit cost price of the product.

-Skimming Pricing: Under this method of pricing the entrepreneur sets a relatively high introductory price for a product or service which he lowers as the demand for the product or service declines.

-Penetration Pricing: This method is applicable when the entrepreneur is confident that by lowering the initial price of the product it can create new customer bases that are using the product or service of competitors. Here the price of the product is lower than similar type of products or services available in the market. It helps in creating a buzz about the product or service.

-Market Rate Policy: Under this method the price set for the product or service is the usual price that is applicable to similar kind of products or services.

-Variable Price Policy: Under this method the price of a product is not same but different at different locations or points of sale.

Market Segmentation

Market segmentation is an attempt to make the marketing strategies customers oriented. It is the activity of grouping of buyers or customers to create a segment. It could be an existing one or a new segment.

Criteria for Market Segmentation:

The following are some of the criteria for creating market segmentation

-Geographical Variables-Here the market segment is made according to geographical areas. For example eastern markets and western markets.

-Demographic Variables-Demographic variables include population variables like age, sex, marital status etc.

-Educational variables: Here the market segmentation is made as per the educational qualification. For example literate and illiterate, under graduates and graduates.

- Income variables-Here the segmentation is made by taking into account the level of income which varies across places, occupation, educational attainment etc.

-Psychological variables-It relates to the psychology of the customers. These are due to personality, lifestyle, tastes, interests etc.

Marketing Mix

Marketing Mix is centred on the 4 Ps of marketing which includes product, price, place and promotion. The business organization uses various marketing tools to foray into the desired market or the desired segment of the market to pursue its marketing objectives. In modern marketing practices a few more Ps are added to the Existing Ps to expand the possibility of attaining marketing objectives. These include People, Process and Physical Environment.

Price indicates as to how much the product is worth. This is a factor of production costs, competition, consumer demographics, supply chain, and pricing strategy.

Product refers to the item or service to be offered sale. It is a combination of performance, features, design and competition.

Place indicates where the product will be sold. This includes online marketing, retail stores or through direct selling.

Promotion refers to creating awareness amongst people regarding the product or service. It includes advertising in media, direct marketing, social media campaigns etc..

Physical environment refers to the market whether a physical storefront presence or creating it's presence felt in the minds of consumers.

Process refers to the system involved in the marketing process.

People includes the individuals supporting the product, either as service providers, marketers, or otherwise.

Industry Analysis- In addition to the market analysis and designing a suitable market, price and customer base an entrepreneur must be well aware about the industry in which he/she intend to continue his/her Business.

Industry consists of a group of Companies which are related based on similar kind of products or services manufactured by them or service provided by them. For example when we say automobile industry it includes all the companies operating in the automobile sector. Industry Analysis helps in understanding the attractiveness of the Industry. Through Industry analysis we can have a broad mapping of the various components that makes an industry either attractive or unattractive to invest. We can gauge the industry from the point of view of buyers, suppliers, new entrants, substitute products and existing participants in the industry.

Thus we can make an analysis of the industry by considering five core factors and can take a decision whether it will be advisable to do a business or not.The first factor that is to be taken into account is the bargaining power of the buyers.If in an industry buyers have a very strong bargaining power which means they can demand to make the prices of the goods and services lower, then that industry cannot be termed attractive. The absence of buyers bargaining power makes the industry attractive, which means the seller can set the prices which suits him to earn a desired amount of profit. The industry in which the sellers are more and the buyers have plenty of options then in such industry the buyers bargaining power is high. Such type of situation occurs in cases where the products are standardized and undifferentiated. In order to avoid such type of situation one may follow the strategy of product differentiation. For example instead of selling a health drink product common to all age groups it could be for working women or for children and may contain added vitamins and minerals.

Similarly if the suppliers of raw materials and components do have the bargaining power then in that case the input price can go up which means the profit will be lowered. The absence of suppliers bargaining power is good for the entrepreneur. Such situation occurs when the numbers of suppliers are less as compared to buyers and there are no other substitute inputs. This will make the industry unattractive to invest.

Similarly the absence of rivalry among competitors is a boon for the entrepreneur whereas if the rivalry is high then it will act as a deterrent. The extent of rivalry among competitors in an Industry affects the competition within that Industry. When the rivalry is weak it will lead to lesser competition and when the rivalry is high the level of competition is higher.

Again one must also look at the substitute products available in the market. Lesser the number of substitute products available in the market better it is for the entrepreneur. The easy availability of substitute products makes an industry less attractive. For example in case of the increase in the price of tea people may substitute it with coffee. Those Industries which have no close substitutes are more attractive than those which have one or more of such substitutes. Thus firms in an Industry having no close substitutes can charge a higher price and earn better returns

Finally the threat of new entrants also plays a vital role in deciding about the attractiveness of the Industry. The industry in which the profitability is high is bound to attract new entrants to the Business. The entry of new entrants to the Business depends on the presence or absence of any barriers to such entry. Barriers to entry could be in the form of Product differentiation, proprietary product technology, favourable location of the Business, easier access to raw materials, economies of scale etc.

Competitor Analysis: The objective of competitor analysis is to define not only who your competitor is but also to have an understanding of who could be potential competitor in future. This will help to face the competition in the market place. A Competitor Analysis is needed to answer the following questions

- With whom should we fight in the Industry and in what sequence
- What is the meaning of the competitor's strategic move and how seriously should we take it.

The entrepreneur must have complete details relating to his competitors. Further all the companies in the industry should not be considered as competitors. For example in the automobile Industry a two-wheeler manufacturer in a strict sense is not a competitor for a four wheeler manufacturer. However in future he may have a plan to expand his product line. Similarly even if the entrepreneur is the business of manufacturing of two wheelers then all the two-wheeler manufacturers will not be considered as competitors. For example if a two wheeler manufacturer is manufacturing a sports bike or a lifestyle bike then his product should not be considered with the manufacturer of an utility or commuter bike. Similarly the scooter manufacturer should not consider a motorcycle manufacturer as his competitor. Similarly a fast-food restaurant should not consider a lifestyle restaurant as its Competitor. Hence it is very important to make a proper competitor analysis after making a proper selection of the Competitor.

Marketing plan: Marketing plan is designed to provide answers to three basic questions:

Where have we been?

It It includes the organization's Strengths and weakness, background of the competition, opportunities and threats in the market place etc.

Where do we want to go in the short run?

The entrepreneur has to ask himself about his short-run goal. The answer may vary from establishing in the market to providing a product through cost effectiveness and cost leadership.

How to get there?

The answer to this will be the type of strategy the entrepreneur may plan. It could be either through cost leadership to product differentiation or could be a combination of both.

Characteristics of a Marketing Plan

(1) It should provide a strategy for accomplishing the company mission or goal.
(2) It should be based on facts and valid assumptions.
(3) An appropriate organization must be designed to implement the marketing plan
(4) It should be short and simple to understand
(5) It should specify performance criteria that will be motivated and controlled.
(6) To become successful the plan should be flexible.
(7) It should provide for continuity so that each annual marketing plan can build on it.

While making a marketing plan it is not enough if one concentrates only on his or her product rather he should find out the number of competitors the Business will have to encounter in the market place. In addition to considering the strength and weakness of his own product the competitor must take a note of the strengths and weaknesses of the the product or service offered by the competitors.

At this point it is important to consider the problems faced by the costumers and what additional services the customer wants over that of the competitor and how to address that situation. The entrepreneur must put himself in the position of the customer to understand his point of view.

At this point the entrepreneur must find out the demand for his goods and services. And he should make it sure that the demand for the product is more than the supply for that product or service. Sometimes although the product supplies are more than the demand the entrepreneur can create a demand for his product by providing some additional features like better quality products, free home delivery and/or providing heavy discounts.

Situation Analysis

At this point the following questions may be answered

What is the Background of the venture?

The answer to this question gives the information regarding the objective of undertaking this particular venture. What is the viability of this project and why the entrepreneur thinks that it will succeed in future?

Strengths and weakness of the venture- The areas of strength and weakness are discussed here. What the uniqueness of this project is as compared to similar other projects and what are the weak points that should be addressed?

Market opportunities and threat- At this point the entrepreneur has to identify the future opportunity that the market holds for his products in future and what will be or can be taken as a threat for the future.

CHAPTER THIRTEEN

Drafting the Projected Financial Statements

Financial planning involves determination in advance of the inflow and outflow of finance for the organization. This requires the preparation of financial budget. Budget is an estimate or plan for any activity. For example cash budget gives an estimate of the cash receipts and payments for a particular period. Budgets could be classified into various categories .When budgets are prepared for a particular period then it could be annual budget, bi-annual budget, quarterly budget, monthly budget and daily budget etc.On the other hand it could also be prepared for various departments or activities or operations.We can classify operational budgets into various categories like Sales Budget, Purchases Budget, Production Budget, Financial Budget etc.

Understanding Working Capital

Working Capital Management involves deciding the amount and composition of current assets and how to finance these current assets.

The main purpose for which working capital is required are as follows:

-To meet the cost of inventories, raw materials purchases, work in process and finished goods etc.

-To pay wages and salaries

-To meet overhead cost, factory cost, office and administration cost, taxes etc.

-To meet selling and distribution expenses, advertising, packaging etc.

What is a Balance Sheet?

A Balance Sheet is a financial Statement which gives information regarding the Assets and Liabilities of a Business. It is prepared for a particular date. For example if it is prepared for 31st March 2020 then in the Balance Sheet it will be mentioned that Balance Sheet of X Ltd.(Name of the Company) for the year ending 31st March,2020.

A Balance Sheet provides all the information relating to the relevant Assets and Liabilities of a particular Business. Assets are the properties owned by the enterprise. Assets could be further subdivided into Fixed Assets and Current Assets. Fixed Assets are basically long-term assets and help the enterprise to earn revenue. It includes land and building, machinery, furnitures and fixtures etc. On the other hand current assets are those assets which are held either in cash or can be converted into cash in short time period. It includes cash in hand, cash at bank, inventories, debtors etc. Similarly Liabilities side of the Balance Sheet shows the owners fund invested in the Business and the money which the enterprise owes to outsiders. These are again of two types. Long-term liabilities and current liabilities. Long–term liabilities include the loans obtained for a longer duration of time and which has to be repaid over a longer period of time. On the other hand current liabilities are those which has to be repaid in shorter period of time. It includes creditors for raw materials and short – term bank loan and bank overdraft.

Balance Sheet of X Ltd. For the Year ended on 31st March 2020

Owners Capital and Outsiders Liability	Amount	Assets	Amount

Owners Capital		Long-Term Assets	
Share Capital		Land	
Reserves & Surplus		Building	
Profit & Loss Account Balance		Office Furniture	
		Plant & Machinery	
Outsiders Liability:		Patent	
Long-Term Secured Loans		Goodwill	
Unsecured Loans		**Current Liabilities**	
Debentures		Debtors	
Current Liabilities:		Raw Materials	
Short-Term Loans		Cash	
Current Creditors			
Bills Payable			
Total		Total	

III. Understanding the Profit & Loss Account

Profit and Loss account explains the profit earned or loss incurred during a particular period. In the statement showing profit or loss the total expenses incurred during a period are deducted from the total revenue earned during that period. Profit incurs if sales revenues during the period are more than the expenses. On the other hand loss takes place if expenses during the period are more than the sales revenues during the period.

A Profit and Loss Account shows items as follows:

Profit & Loss Account for the Year ended March 31st 2020

Particulars	Amount	Particulars	Amount

To Gross Loss b/d To Salaries To Office Rent To Printing & Stationery To Insurance To Audit fees To electricity charges To Discount Allowed To Bank Charges To Interest Payment To Loss on Sale of Asset To Depreciation To Advertisement Exp. To Net Profit b/d		By Gross Profit b/d By Commission Received By Interest Received By Rent Received By Dividend Received By Profit on Sale of Assets By Interest received on Debentures By Net Loss b/d	

IV. Preparing a Cash flow Statement-Cash flow statement explains the actual inflow and outflow of cash from operating, financing and investing activities during a period. It does not include any fictitious items and portrays the actual figure of cash outflows and inflows.

In a Business Organisation Cash is generated from any or a combination of more than one of the following activities
- ☐ Operating Activities
- ☐ Investing Activities
- ☐ Financing Activities

Operating Activities include the following:
- ☐ Cash received from Sale of Goods and Services
- ☐ Cash received from Fees, Commission and Royalties etc.
- ☐ Cash paid to Suppliers for goods and services
- ☐ Cash paid to and on behalf of employees

Cash flows from Investing Activities include the following:
- ☐ Cash paid for purchase of fixed assets

- ☐ Cash received from sale of fixed assets
- ☐ Cash paid for purchase of shares and debentures
- ☐ Cash received from the sale of Shares and debentures
- ☐ Cash loans and Advances

Cash flows from financing activities include the following
- ☐ Cash proceeds from the issue of shares and Debentures
- ☐ Repayment of borrowed funds in Cash

Statement of Cashflows of X Ltd. for the year ending on 31st March 2020		
	Current Year	Previous Year
Cash flows from Operating activities		
Cash receipt from Customers	xxxxx	xxxxx
Cash Paid to Suppliers and employees	xxxxx	xxxxx
Cash generated from Operations	xxxxx	xxxxx
Net Cash from Operating Activities	xxxxx	xxxxx
Cash Flows from Investing Activities		
Business acquisitions-Net of Cash Aquired	xxxxx	xxxxx
Purchase of property, plant and equipment	xxxxx	xxxxx
Net Cash used in investing Activities	xxxxx	xxxxx
Cash flows from Financing Activities		
Proceeds from issue of Share Capital	xxxxx	xxxxx
Proceeds from Long Term Borrowings	xxxxx	xxxxx
Payment of Long-term Borrowings	xxxxx	xxxxx
Net Cash used in Financing Activities	xxxxx	xxxxx
Net increase in Cash and Cash Equivalents	xxxxx	xxxxx
Cash and Cash Equivalents at end of Period	xxxxx	xxxxx

V. Understanding Various Financial Ratios: The following are some of the important ratios and relevant for the preparation of a

Business Plan.
- Liquidity ratios
- Leverage ratios
- Activity ratios
- Profitability ratios

Liquidity Ratios: Liquidity ratios measure a firm's ability to meet it's current obligations or liabilities. Some of the important ratios relevant for understanding a Business plan are as follows:

Current Ratio = Current Assets/Current Liabilities

Liquid Ratios = (Current Assets- Inventories)/Current Liabilities

Leverage Ratios: Leverage Ratios also known as Capital Structure Ratios is a measure of the long-term financial viability of a firm. It measures the relationship between the funds provided by the owners and that of the outsiders.

Debt-Equity Ratio: Total Debt/Net Worth

Activity ratios: These ratios evaluate the efficiency with which the firm manages and utilizes its assets. These ratios, thus, involve a relationship between sales and assets.

Inventory Turnover = Cost of Goods Sold/Average Inventory

Debtors Turnover = Credit Sales/ Average Debtors

Profitability Ratios: These ratios are calculated to measure the operating efficiency of a company.

Gross Profit Ratio= Gross Profit/Sales x 100

Net Profit Margin = EBIT(1-T)/Sales

Earnings Per Share(EPS)= Profit After Tax/ Total no. of Shares

Price-Earnings Ratio = Market Price per Share/EPS

VI. Break even Analysis: Breakeven point is the figure or number at which point of production the firm does not earn any profit. Any number of units produced beyond this point will result in a profit for the business where as any number of productions below this unit will result in a loss for the Business .Hence the figure should be a lower one in order to make the business more viable.

CHAPTER FOURTEEN

ENTREPRENEURIAL STRATEGIES

As discussed in earlier chapters there are various reasons for taking a decision regarding embarking on an entrepreneurial career. The reasons could range from workplace disturbance to the urge to become the master of one's own Business. However, it's not enough to start a Business. Unless and otherwise proper strategies are adopted the survival of the Business becomes difficult because of the Competition in the marketplace. So it is important for entrepreneurs to develop strategies for survival and growth of their Business. Some of the strategies that the entrepreneur should keep in mind are as follows:

Growth

The growth of an entrepreneurial venture can relate to its full utilization of unutilized resources of the firm. As a start-up though entrepreneurial firms are short of financial resources but they are full of entrepreneurial drive and can develop new ways to grow in the market place. These strategies are unconventional and most of the times goes unnoticed by the larger competitors. They can use speed and stealth in a very unconventional manner and can create disruption in the market place by following a guerrilla strategy. However various instances from the past points out that entrepreneurs suffer heavy losses by becoming over confident and these should be avoided at all cost and the entrepreneurs should protect themselves against taking high risks.

Innovation

Though Innovation is closely associated with entrepreneurship but it could be used as a form of strategy. Innovation as a strategy offers various advantages. First of all, firms introducing innovative products earn super-normal profits for certain period so long as the competitors do not emerge. Further firms coming up with disruptive technologies erase the competitor's advantages and try to dictate the terms. Innovation should not be thought of from technological point of view only. It may be the new way of using an existing product or service or it could also relate to innovative methods of production or doing work which can give competitive advantage.

Network

Network Strategy refers to the use of connections and relations at the personal level and organizational level in order to gain the volume of the Business. As most of the new entrepreneurial firms do not have a strong track record and as they are yet to develop a complete plan so far as their products and services are concerned hence have to rely on their existing network of friends, relatives, colleagues and associates. However in order to be successful the entrepreneur must not take his network for granted and must try to prove the positivity of these advantages. As these networks can create successful opportunities hence the ability to create a good network can be beneficial to the successful existence of the entrepreneurial venture.

Harvest and Exit

The Strategic decision-making process for entrepreneurial ventures is composed of the following eight interrelated steps:

1.Develop the Basic Business Idea

2.Scan and assess the external environment

3.Scan and assess the internal factors

4.Analyze the Strategic Factors

5.Generate a Business Plan

6.Implement the Business Plan

7, Evaluate the Strategy

CHAPTER FIFTEEN

Sample Business Plan of an Amusement Park

EXECUTIVE SUMMARY

I. Project On:	Amusement Park
II. Covered Area:	100 Acres
III. Land & Equipment :	270 Lakhs
IV. Power Requirement :	50 KW
V. Employment Potential:	70
VI. Break-Even Point :	42%
VII. Location :	Bhubaneswar(India)
VIII. Expected Turnover(1st Year):	72 Lakhs
IX. PBIT(1st Year) :	42 Lakhs
X. Technology :	Indegenious
XI. Total Capital Requirement:	305 Lakhs

Basis and Presumptions

1. The project profile has been prepared on the basis of the 25 working days in a month.

2. It is presumed that during the first year the capacity

utilization will be 75% followed by 85% during the next year and 100% in subsequent years.

3. Depreciation on machinery and equipments has been taken @10%.

4. The rates given for salaries and wages for the skilled workers and others are on the basis of the minimum rate prevailing in the state.

5. The rates given for machinery, equipments, and raw materials are those prevailing at the time of the preparation of the project profile and are likely to vary from place to place and supplier to supplier.

6. It is expected that the project will become operational in 6-7 months' time..

Vision Statement

To passionately promote peace, love and oneness through educational and inspirational activities, thrilling rides and entertaining games.

To foster positive mental and physical Development and the renewing of mind in a relaxed environment.

Mission Statement

To Create a Peaceful, friendly, quality environment to foster love, family, unity and friendships through recreation, leisure and entertainment for the well-being of individuals and families.

Goals: To Create a Benchmark in Customer Service.

Objectives: To make the project fully operational and profitable in next two years time.

Industry Analysis:

Looking from the Competition point of view the rivalry is not very high among the Competitors as it is a Concept and hence product differentiation exists as no two Competitors services are same.

Substitute products are available hence Buyers bargaining power is there.

Since the input materials are available in plenty hence the bargaining power of Supplier is very low

As it is a Capital intensive Project and it is a Concept hence the threat of new entrants is low.

Competitor Analysis:

At present locally there are no Competitors. But globally the Competition is high. Hence at first we will try to take advantage of the local monopoly and will gradually cater to the increased global market.

Market Promotion

- ☐ Online Advertising
- ☐ Newspapers
- ☐ Hoardings
- ☐ Social Media
- ☐ Sponsoring various events

SWOT Analysis

Strength

The strength the project lies in the fact that Amusement parks are very much in demand in today's generation. Exposure to television and internet has made people aware about such type of theme parks elsewhere in the world.

The project does not require too much inventories because of the fact that it is basically a service organization.

As it has a fast cash cycle hence the working capital will not be tied up for a very long period.

Weakness

The project suffers from the following limitation.

1. Peoples spending habits are not clearly known.
2. The cash flow during the rainy months will be low.

Opportunities

1. As there are few Competitors in the Market place, hence the market potential of the Project is very high.

2. The Project has the capacity to attract foreign exchange.

Threat

Since the project does not require too much technical expertise, hence Competitors may step in to take advantage of it.

ABOUT THE PROJECT

Amusement parks and theme parks are terms for a collection of rides and other entertainment attractions assembled for the purpose of entertaining a large group of people. An amusement park is more elaborate than a simple city park or playground, usually providing attractions meant to cater to children, teenagers, and adults.

The twin city of Bhubaneswar and Cuttack is growing at a very fast pace both in terms of the population as well as the area. Compared to a decade ago, people's standard of living has increased much because of the expansion of the economic activity. Consequently peoples' spending pattern has also increased. They prefer to spend more amounts on leisure and amusement. People are also more increasingly looking for leisure and amusement activities .In this context the Amusement Park has increased importance.

The twin city of Bhubaneswar and Cuttack and its surrounding places lack such type of specialized amusement parks. Thus there is more need of such type of projects in the Twin City.

In order to understand the need and profitability of such type of projects a questionnaire is prepared and a survey is made amongst the park goers of the Twin City.

Proposal

The proposed Amusement Park is a unique project of its kind. Of late peoples spending habit has been changed. Due to increasing middle class income and increase in the communication network such type of projects is gaining importance. People prefer to spend some of their disposable income in quality entertainments. The increase in the number of malls in metro cities, increase in luxury resorts and luxury satellite towns are examples of this.

This is further accentuated by the liberalization policy adopted by Govt. and the vast increase in communication networks. The no. of flights to Bhubaneswar over the year has increased. Further over the years the no. of workplace and offices of various Software, FMCG and other Corporate have increased in Bhubaneswar . This means again increase in the disposable income and more number of affluent people including the company personnel. Again the increase in the telecommunication network, the availability of World Wide Web means that there is easy access to the internet. Thus the company can promote itself in telecom networks as well as on the internet.

The proposed project will be situated near Phulanakhra/Puri which will be an ideal place for number of reasons. First of all it is situated near N.H.-5. It is nearer to the City of Bhubaneswar which is well connected both by rail and air. Since it is well connected, hence it is an ideal spot for setting up an amusement park.

Techno-Economic Viability Study Report of Fun City Ltd.

1. Background

Fun City Limited is planning to set up a project for Amusement Park in the outskirts of the City of Bhubaneswar.
The cost of project estimated at Rs.305 lakhs.
The Company proposes to go for external financial
assistance by way of fresh Term Loan of Rs. 100.00 lakhs
and Working Capital borrowing of Rs. 35 lakhs

The balance will be contributed by promoters.

2. Background Of The Promoters

There are three promoters involved in the project. The main Promoter is an NRI having experience in Hospitality Industry. The other promoters are local Businessmen and mainly investors and will not have any active involvement in Business.

The Company will be registered in the name of Fun City Ltd.

3. Project Details

I. About the Amusement Park

Fun City Ltd proposes to start amusement park in the Twin-City of Bhubaneswar and Cuttack to provide recreation and amusement activities to the people. The Park will cater to the requirements of all the age group including Children, youngsters as well as adults. The Park also includes Water Sports in the Water Park. The equipments installed in the Park includes Climbers, Water Playing Slide, Joy Rides, Multi Lanes, Float Rides, Tornado, Rope Way etc.

It is expected that the Park will attract more than 5, 00,000 visitors per annum..

II. Land & Premises.

The company has procured around 100 Acres of land for this purpose and is also in the process of acquiring more lands in the adjacent areas to the Amusement Park. The infrastructure of the project is on the verge of completion and the park is slated to open by the end of the financial year.

III. Rides & Attractions Equipment

The following items of plant and machinery has been proposed to be installed section-wise:

List of Equipment	Estimated Cost (Rs.)

Children's Climbers	0.50 Lakhs
Water Playing Slide	9.00 Lakhs
Joy Rides	8.50 Lakhs
Multi Lanes	12.00 Lakhs
Float Rides	10.00 Lakhs
Tornado	30.00 Lakhs
Rope Way	50.00 Lakhs

The cost of plant and machinery has been estimated at Rs. 120 lakhs.

The promoter is yet to submit quotation / other documents of individual items in support of the cost of plant and machinery provided in the cost of project. Since cost of the individual items of the above are not backed by supporting documents like quotations etc., the same has to be submitted before disbursement of term loan in the event that the proposal for term loan is considered for sanction.

V. Electrical Installations, Furniture & Fixture and Misc. Equipments.

The documents for installations like transformers, generators will be submitted before disbursement of term loan.

VII. Maintenance Dept.

Power

The power requirement is to the extent of 50 KW. The company has deposited security money to the concerned authorities for obtaining the requisite power load.

Water

Water is mainly used for cooling the water circulation system. Make up water will be needed to cover the evaporation of water in the cooling tower. The requirement of water has been estimated at around 400 Litres per day. Water shall be available from Tanks as well as Tube-Wells to be sunk in the unit.

VIII. Manpower Requirement:

The following manpower has been proposed for the unit:

DESIGNATION	NO	SALARY	TOTAL
Park Manager	1	10,000.00	10,000.00
Electrician	2	5,000.00	10,000.00
Supervisor	3	5000.00	15,000.00
Machine Operator	3	5000.00	15,000.00
Skilled Worker	10	4,000.00	40,000.00
Unskilled Worker	20	3,000.00	60,000.00
Accounts Clerk	2	5,000.00	10,000.00
Peon/Guard	4	2,500.00	10,000.00
Total Salary Per Month			170,000.00
Salary Per Annum			20,40,000.00

4. Project Cost and Means of Finance of a Proposed Amusement Park (Fun City Ltd.)

	RS. IN LAKHS
PROJECT COST:	
I. LAND & PREMISES	150 Lakhs
II. EQUIPMENT	
1. Children Climbers	0.50 Lakhs

2. Water Playing Slide   9.00 Lakhs
3. Joy Rides   8.50 Lakhs
4. Multi Lanes   12.00 Lakhs
5. Float Rides   10.00 Lakhs
6. Tornado   30.00 Lakhs
7. Rope Way   50.00 Lakhs

Total   **120 Lakhs**

III. WORKING CAPITAL REQUIREMENTS: 35.00 Lakhs

TOTAL PROJECT COST   : **305.00 Lakhs**

MEANS OF FINANCING

Equity   :

PROMOTERS CONTRIBUTION :   70 Lakhs
INDIAN PUBLIC (10 lakhs shares @ of Rs. 10/share) : 100 Lakhs
WORKING CAPITAL LOAN   :   35 Lakhs
TERM LOAN FROM BANK   :   100 Lakhs
TOTAL   :   **305 Lakhs**

5. PROJECT IMPLEMENTATION SCHEDULE:

The implementation of the project includes various jobs such as procurement of technical know-how, transfer of technology, market Surveys, preparation of the project report, selection of site, financing of the project, procurement of equipment, recruitment of staff, erection of equipments, trial production and commercial production etc. Project implementation will take a period of 7-8 months from the date of approval of the scheme.

Break-up of activities, with relative time for each activity is shown below:

ACTIVITY   **PERIOD**

1. Scheme Preparation — 1 Month

2. Sanction of Loan — 2-5 Month

3. Clearance from State Pollution Control Board — 3-4 Month

4. Placement of Order for Equipment — 4-5 Month

5. Installation of Equipment — 5-6 Months

6. Power Connection — 3-5 Month

7. Trial Run — 6-7 Month

8. Commercial Run — 7-8 Month

PROJECTED BALANCE SHEET OF FUN CITY LTD.

RS. IN LAKHS

	Year 1	Year 2	Year 3	Year 4	Year 5
A. SOURCES OF FUNDS					
EQUITY SHARE CAPITAL	170 Lakhs	170 Lakhs	170 Lakhs	170 Lakhs	170 Lakhs
RESERVES & SURPLUS	15 Lakhs	35 Lakhs	40 Lakhs	50 Lakhs	60 Lakhs
- PROFIT & LOSS					
TOTAL SHAREHOLDERS FUNDS	185 Lakhs	205 Lakhs	210 Lakhs	220 Lakhs	230 Lakhs
OTHERS (SPECIFY ITEM WISE)	35 Lakhs	30 Lakhs	25 Lakhs	20 Lakhs	15 Lakhs
1. Working Capital Loan	100 Lakhs	90 Lakhs	80 Lakhs	70 Lakhs	60 Lakhs
2. Term Loan From Banks	320 Lakhs	325 Lakhs	315 Lakhs	310 Lakhs	305 Lakhs
TOTAL	270 Lakhs	300 Lakhs	270 Lakhs	240 Lakhs	210 Lakhs
B.	27 Lakhs	30 Lakhs	30 Lakhs	30 Lakhs	30 Lakhs
C. **APPLICATION**	243 Lakhs	270 Lakhs	240 Lakhs		

OF FUNDS:					
GROSS FIXED ASSETS		5 Lakhs	5 Lakhs	210 Lakhs	180 Lakhs
LESS: DEPRECIATION (10%SLM)		15 Lakhs	15 Lakhs	5 Lakhs	5 Lakhs
NET FIXED ASSETS (a)	57 Lakhs	82 Lakhs	112 Lakhs	15 Lakhs	15 Lakhs
OTHERS (SPECIFY ITEM WISE)	30 Lakhs	5 Lakhs	5 Lakhs	167 Lakhs	232 Lakhs
DIVIDEND PAID (b)	87 Lakhs	87 Lakhs	117 Lakhs	10 Lakhs	5 Lakhs
REPAYMENT OF LOAN (c)	40 Lakhs	72 Lakhs	87 Lakhs	177 Lakhs	237 Lakhs
CASH & BANK BALANCES	47 Lakhs	15 Lakhs	30 Lakhs	132 Lakhs	177 Lakhs
OTHER CURRENT ASSETS	320 Lakhs	325 Lakhs	315 Lakhs	45 Lakhs	60 Lakhs
TOTAL CURRENT ASSETS				310 Lakhs	305 Lakhs
TOTAL CURRENT LIBILITIES					
NET CURRENT ASSETS (CA-CL) (d)					
TOTAL (a+b+c+d)					

Interpretation –

➤ The net worth of the company has increased from Rs. 185 lakhs in the financial year 1 to 230 lakhs in the year 5 (Δ in % is about 25 %), which shows an increase in the book value per share.

➤ At the same time the debt burden of the company has also decreased consistently.

➤ The dividend paid to the shareholders has been maintained at a constant rate, which shows the confidence of the promoters in the project.

Projected Profit & Loss Statement (Fig in Lakhs)

Particulars	Year 1	Year 2	Year 3	Year 4	Year 5
Revenue					
Income from sale of tickets	30	50	55	55	70
Income from sale of food items	20	30	30	35	40
Income from sale of merchandise	22	30	30	40	40
Total (a)	72	110	115	130	150
Operational Expenditure					
Maintenance expenses	3	4	5	4	4
Salaries	10	12	12	14	15
Electricity	2	3	3	4	4
Administrative expenses	1	1.5	1	1.5	2
Advertisement & promotional	12	15	16	19	22
Miscellaneous	2	4.5	3	2.5	3
Total (b)	30	40	40	45	50
Op. Profit (a - b)	42	70	75	85	100
Less:					
Depreciation	27	30	30	30	30
Profit	15	40	45	55	65
Dividend	Nil	5	5	5	5
Transfer to reserves	15	35	40	50	60

The profit and loss statement shows that the total revenue of the company has been increasing consistently over the years. Over a period of 5 years the total revenue is doubled from Rs. 72 lakhs in the year 1 to 150 lakhs in the year 5. Consequently the operating profit has also increased from 42 lakhs in the year 1 to Rs. 100 lakhs in the year 5.

The company is maintaining a constant dividend policy and transferring the balance of the P/L A/C to reserve and surplus A/C. The reserve is expected to increase from 15 lakhs in the year 2011-12 to 60 lakhs in the year 2015-16. As a future prospect the company can always fall back on the internal source of finance for further expansion of the business.

IMPORTANT RATIOS   RS. IN LAKHS

	1ST YEAR	2ND YEAR	3RD YEAR	4TH YEAR	5TH YEAR
CURRENT RATIO	2.175	1.42	2	3.25	2
CASH RATIO	0.75	0.57	0.83	1.75	0.75
DEBT/EQUITY	0.79	0.70	0.61	0.52	0.44
OP. PROFIT/INCOME	58%	63%	65%	65%	66%
RETURN ON TOTAL ASSETS	4.6%	12.3%	14.2%	17.7%	21.3%
RONW/ROI	8.1%	19.5%	21.4%	25%	28.2%
EPS (RS.)	0.88	2.35	2.64	3.23	3.82

BREAK EVEN ANALYSIS   RS. IN LAKHS

	1ST YEAR	2ND YEAR	3RD YEAR	4TH YEAR	5TH YEAR
GROSS REVENUE	72 Lakhs	110 Lakhs	115 Lakhs	130 Lakhs	150 Lakhs
VARIABLE EXPENSES (SPECIFY ITEMWISE)	20 Lakhs	30 Lakhs	30 Lakhs	35 Lakhs	40 Lakhs
CONTRIBUTIONS	52 Lakhs	80 Lakhs	85 Lakhs	95 Lakhs	110 Lakhs
P/V RATIO	72.22%	72.22%	73.91%	75.38%	73.33%
FIXED EXPENSES (SPECIFY ITEMWISE)	10 Lakhs	15 Lakhs	20 Lakhs	20 Lakhs	20 Lakhs
PROFIT	42 Lakhs	65 Lakhs	65 Lakhs	75 Lakhs	90 Lakhs
BREAK-EVEN POINT	30	45	45	45	60

Cash Flow Statement

A. Cash Flow from Operating Activities

	Year 1	Year 2	Year 3	Year 4	Year 5
	Lakhs	Lakhs	Lakhs	Lakhs	Lakhs
Net Profit before Taxation	15	40	45	85	100
Add: Adjustment for Depreciation	27	30	30	30	30
Operating Profit	42	70	75	115	130
Adjustment for Direct Taxes Paid	05	10	10	25	30
Operating profit before W.C Changes	37	60	65	95	100
Working Capital Changes	----	42	(15)	(15)	(15)
Total of A	37	102	50	75	85

B. Cash Flow from Investing Activities

	Year 1	Year 2	Year 3	Year 4	Year 5
Purchase of Fixed Assets	(270)	(57)	-	-	-
Total of B	(270)	(57)	-	-	-

C. Cash Flow from Financing Activities

	Year 1	Year 2	Year 3	Year 4	Year 5
Repayment of Loan	(15)	(15)	(15)	(15)	(15)
Dividend Paid		(5)	(5)	(5)	(5)
Proceeds from Issue of Shares	170				
-Unsecured Loans	135	-	-	-	-
Total of C	290	(20)	(20)	(20)	(20)
Net Cash Flow during the Year (A+B+C)	57	25	30	55	65

Cash Balance at the beginning	0	57	82	112	167
Cash Balance at the end	57	82	112	167	232

Current Ratio

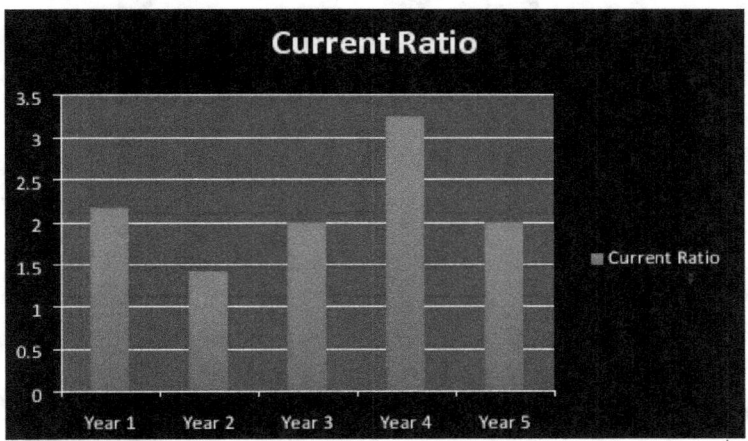

The current ratio position of the company during the 1st year is satisfactory. as it is more than the required rate of return i.e. more than 2:1 However in the 2nd year, it has declined which implies that the firm has diverted its working capital to purchase some fixed assets however this position has improved from 3rd year on words.

The average current ratio of the propose firm is 2.169 which indicates that the firm is able to meet its current obligations as and when it becomes due thus able to meet the confidence of creditors

Absolute Liquid Ratio

The absolute liquid of the firm is more than satisfactory since it is above the bankers, rule of thumb i.e. 0.5:1. However during the 4th year of its operation it is very high which indicates that the firm could have better utilized its idle funds and could have got more return from its funds.

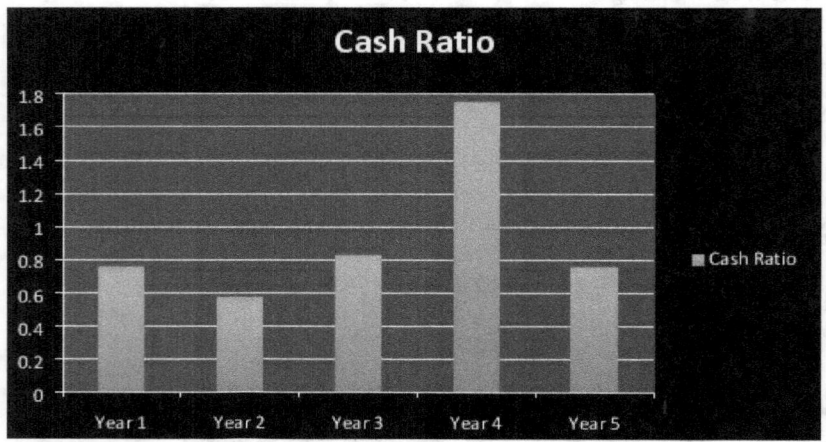

Debt/Equity Ratio

The debt equity ratio is more than satisfactory because in the short run the firm need not have to pay interest. This analysis indicates that this firm is following a conservative funding policy. However the firm could get benefit from the fact that it is a low leveraged firm. Hence it could get more funds in future for the purpose of expansion of business.

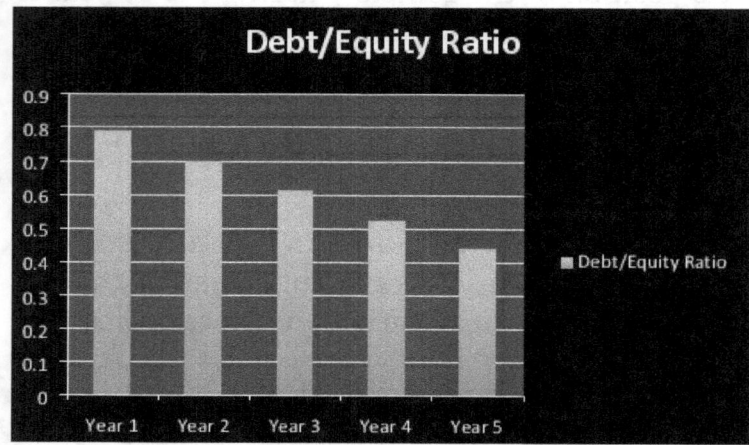

Operating Profit/Sales Ratio

This ratio indicates that the firm is able to have a higher margin of safety and it could attain profitability even at a lower level of sales volume. Profitability of the firm is more than the industry average.

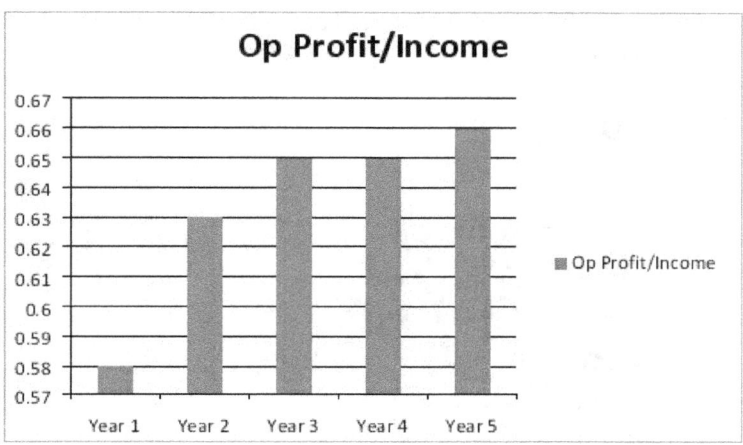

Return of Total Assets.

This ratio is low during the 1st year of the operation compared to the later years. It indicates that from 3rd year onwards the firm is able to get a fair return on its assets thus benefiting its share holders.

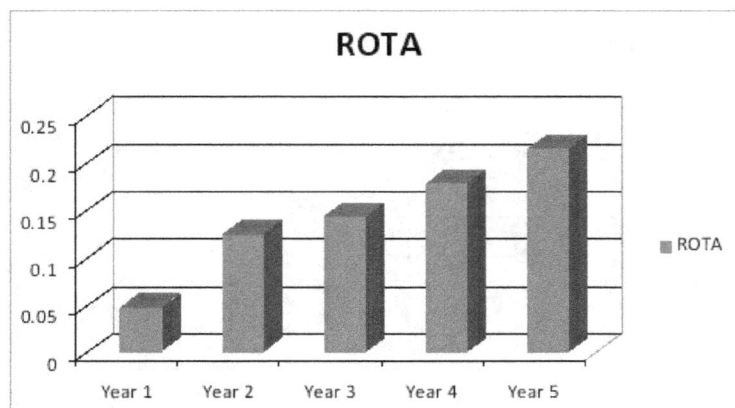

Return On Net Worth

Return on net worth is increasing over the life of the project, which will increase the confidence of the share holders. It is showing a steady growth rate. This will attract the potential investors.

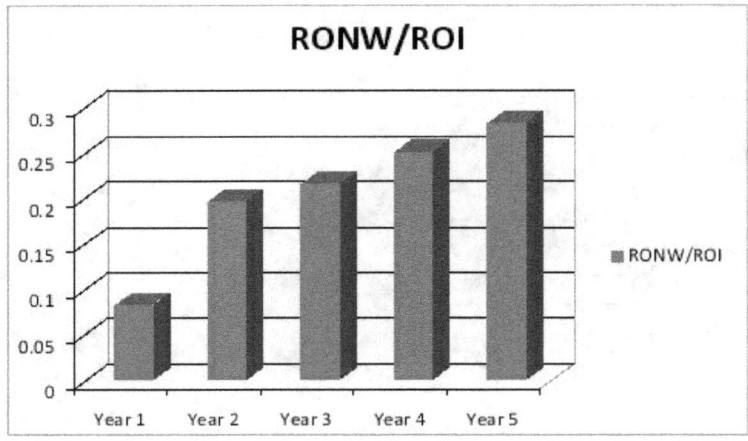

Earnings Per Share

Earnings per share is showing an upward trend. This will increase the market of the shares. The share's of the company will be much in demand in the capital market.

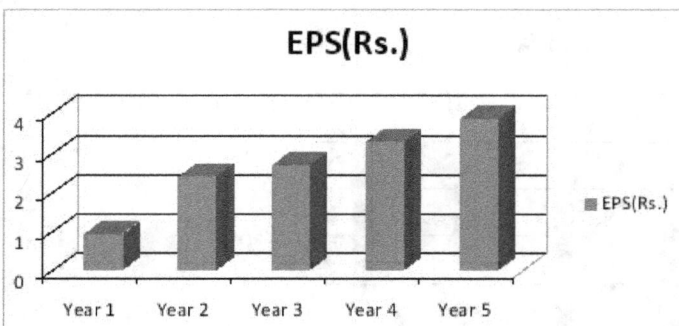

Cost Volume Profit Analysis

The break-even point analysis of the company indicates that the company is able to attain profit at a lower level of operation. The average P/V ratio of the company is more than 72 %.

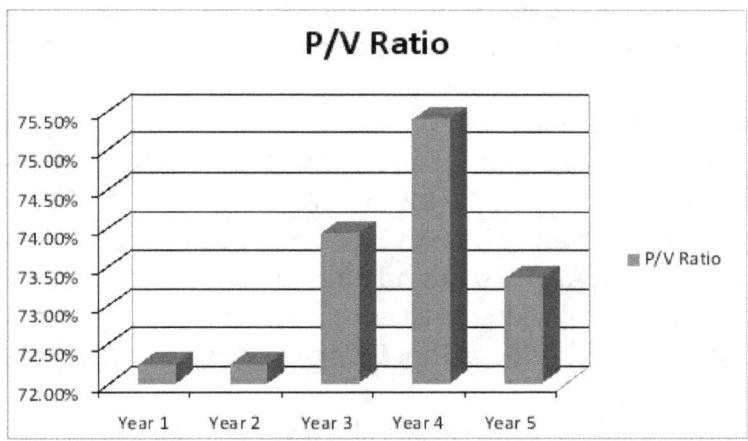

Viability Report

- Easy Accessibility of Land
- Increase in purchasing power of the people
- Unsaturated market
- Easy availability of Equipment
- Tourism & Golden Triangle
- Twin city advantage:
  - Existence of urban class & relative purchasing power
  - Close proximity, access and comfort
- The commercial operation from the project is envisaged from April 2021.
- Based on the assumptions made the profitability has been worked out from 2021-22 to 2025-26.
- The repayment of Term Loan has been proposed to commence from April 2021 and end on March 2030.
- The Company expects to earn a profit of Rs. 42 Lakhs in the first year of its operation. The break-even point in the first year of operation is 42% of sales.
- Trend % of sales and profit shows an increasing trend which makes the offer even more lucrative.

www.ingramcontent.com/pod-product-compliance
Lightning Source LLC
Chambersburg PA
CBHW060852220526
45466CB00003B/1339